LIFT YOUR FAMILY OUT OF CHAOS

HOW TO LIVE WITH, SCHEDULE AND ORGANIZE YOUR ADHD FAMILY OF COLLECTORS, HOARDERS AND PROCRASTINATORS

Wendy Keenan Myers

Published by Ask the Landlady

Marietta, Ohio

©2024 Ask the Landlady LLC

All rights reserved.

Library of Congress Control Number: 2023924637

The author and publisher have taken reasonable precautions in the preparation of this book and believe the facts presented in the book are accurate as of the publication date. However, neither the author nor the publisher assumes any responsibility for any errors or omissions. The author and publisher disclaim any liability resulting from the use or application of the information contained in this book and the information is not intended to serve as financial, legal, or other business advice related to individual situations.

No part of this book may be reproduced, stored in a retrieval system, or transmitted by any means, electronic, mechanical, photocopying, recording or otherwise, without written permission from the copyright holder.

Dedication

To all organized people everywhere. Your superpower is staying on schedule and getting things done. It's both a curse and a blessing. Choose today to embrace the blessing.

Most organizational books are written by people who fall into one of two categories: professional organizing expert or former slob-turned-internet sensation organizing expert. The books written by these two different camps target the poor soul who is drowning in mess and need their expertise. But let's face it, the people who are drowning in chaos don't have the time nor the inclination to read a book about how to organize the junk drawer or the spice cabinet. So, these books end up getting read by the most organized family member who is seeking order for the home. That person does not need to be talked into organization and he or she certainly does not need all the tips, tricks, and checklists. The people who **need** the information are the friends, coworkers and family members who annoy the organized person with messy and disorganized lives. However, the collectors, hoarders and procrastinators are never going to seek out this information; they have more fun things to do. Instead of trying to reach the organizationally lost souls, this book aims to help **the organized one who is just trying to tamp down the chaos he or she sees all around—the same person who tries endlessly to organize the lives of those they live with.**

In this book, Wendy Keenan Myers, an accomplished real estate investor and CEO of Ask the Landlady, outlines a gentle perspective on how to gain buy-in from the family when tackling the monumental goal of streamlining your house organization and creating systems of time management and efficiency that even your most ADHD family members can follow.

TABLE OF CONTENTS

Introduction   7
Organizational Personality Traits   11
   Specific Personality Situations   17
A Word or Two About Hoarding and Collecting   23
   Why are collectors so into stuff?   28
   What Are the Specific Concerns of Collectors?   31
**A Word or Two About ADHD,
Defiance and Procrastination**   37
   ADHD Attributes   38
   Reasons You Might be Encountering Opposition   41
   Common Procrastination Outlooks   45
   Personality Viewpoints   50
How to Get Started   57
Don't Get Rid of Anything   71
If You Don't Schedule It, It Will Never Happen   77
**Time to Deploy the Troops and Utilize
Different Organizational Strategies to Control Clutter**   81
   Do You Still Love It? (The "Spark Joy" Approach)   83
   The Valuable Real Estate Approach   85
   The Pareto Principle or the 80/20 Rule   89
   The Creation of a Personal Oasis Approach   90
   The Hand Holding or Companionship Approach   96

The Tackle the Scary First Approach	100
The First Responder Approach	103
The Embrace the Clutter Approach	105
The Little and Often Approach	112

Helping Your Family Create and Maintain Their Own Schedules — **125**

Maintain Multiple Calendars	126
Create and Maintain ONE Family Calendar	128
Develop Personalized Reminder Systems	129
Create Specific Prompts	136
Consider Utilizing the Pomodoro Technique	139
Do the Hardest Task First	141
Break Tasks Down into a Step-by-Step Process	143
Eliminate Busy Work from Your Daily Routine	145
Create a Tickler File or 43 Folders® System	150
Figure Out a Way to Deal with Your In-Box	152
Deploy a Body Doubling or Mirroring Technique	157
Institute a Set Weekly Family Routine	159
Keep a running project list	160

Let's Make This Fun — **167**

Show Me the Money — **171**

Venues for Selling Items	173

Dealing with Difficult Organizational Situations — **179**

Staying On Track — **191**

Book and Website Resources — **197**

INTRODUCTION

Before The Vaccination and very early during the COVID 19 pandemic, my husband contracted COVID from working at the hospital and started to get sick when we were out of town. The previous week he had gotten the flu vaccination and thought that he was just feeling the ill effects of the shot. He had also been burning the midnight oil with work and thought he was just run down. Just about the time we realized that we probably both had this new virus that no one knew anything about (wow, I can't taste this whisky; it's like drinking water!), Todd started having breathing problems. Full disclosure, Todd is a doctor so that means he is a terrible patient. He tried resting and inhalers and the best doctor cure-all and answer for every ailment: Ibuprofen. All to no avail—he ended up hospitalized after a harrowing trip to the ER when his breathing got so bad, he couldn't keep his head up. Long story short—I ended up in a hotel room out of town in Atlanta while Todd stayed for eight days at Emory University Hospital ICU, fighting for air. Luckily, all ended well. Todd broke out of the hospital early (again, doctors are the worst patients!), we quarantined for another couple weeks and then he was back to somewhat normal living.

But in the midst of Todd being in the hospital and me being alone in a hotel room, I was in deep despair. I wasn't sure if Todd was going to make it; people were dying all around him on the COVID floor. I was alone in a hotel room with this new frightening virus and away from all my family members. My 17-year-old daughter was in between cancer treatments for leukemia (hence why we were on a short rest and relaxation trip out of town), and I was afraid of missing out on helping her through the next round, though I was thankful we didn't infect her before we left on our trip. In the middle of despair, all I could do was watch comfort television. And for me, it was *The Home Edit* on Netflix. I love those women—I love the rainbow style of organization. ROYGBIV is the best. I love the clean living, the purging, the orderliness of it all. My amazing, supportive friends sent me their book while I was incarcerated at the Marriott hotel, and I pored over the glossy pages and dreamed of a pantry with labeled clear containers and a refrigerator with decanted juices. Yes, it was very indulgent and entitled, but again, I was sad and lonely and feverish with COVID.

I vowed right then and there—if we make it through all of this—Leukemia and COVID— I was going to get our house in order. And by order, I meant MY order, a beautiful clean landscape of home with everything labeled and all beautiful. Well—we made it—thank you God!—the cancer treatments worked, Todd recovered, and we got back on track. And we came out of the experiences with better understanding and patience with each other. And so, I came to another epiphany—my vision of order was NOT going to work with my family, my fantastic, hoarding, ADHD personality family.

And so began a journey to organize the home even though I am married to a hard-core collector and even though my youngest child is off the charts with her ADHD—complicated with chemotherapy brain (yes, it is a real thing, you can Google it). And I realized that we had already been on this journey—we had been making concessions to each other all along and I hadn't realized it. So, with some self-reflection and tweaking of our ideas, here's my journey to home and life organization that mostly satisfies everyone. I've written it all down here because this is the book that I wish I could have read years earlier. This information would have saved a lot of hurt feelings, daily annoyances, and misunderstandings. My family is nowhere near perfect, but we get things done and we have a lot of fun along the way, even though we have very different attitudes towards daily organization and scheduling.

Disclaimer: I am not a trained professional in psychology or psychiatry. The ideas in this book come from my personal experience with family, friends and coworkers along with extensive research into various organizational and scheduling systems.

(1)

ORGANIZATIONAL PERSONALITY TRAITS

When you grow up living in a trailer park, like me, you learn to minimize stuff. If something new comes into your little matchbox room, then something must go out to make room for the newbie. It is a constant buy and purge cycle that works well for people who enjoy holding yard sales and taking things to donate to Goodwill. That's me. It does not work well if you like to hold onto stuff — if you think you might use that item someday or want to have it on hand to give to your children or use it for a Halloween costume. That's my husband. He didn't grow up during the Depression, but he likes to hold onto any tool he might need in the future or any piece of clothing that he might fit into one day. Once he realizes an item has no use for his life, he wants to sell it for a premium price. No matter that I look at the item and say it is a 50 cents yard sale item, he is convinced that it will garner $25 from someone who would appreciate the item as much as he does. And don't get me started on our ADHD child who has too many pairs of shoes and stuff exploded all over her bedroom—and who is always on a quest to find some lost object.

Wendy Keenan Myers

It is easy to think that everyone has the same mind set and I have made this mistake too often. This faulty thinking either results in me (1) throwing away some scrap of paper that had a monumentally important phone number, thus ensuring a major argument or (2) enabling my child by completely organizing her backpack or study area, thus leading to the creation of a child who cannot follow my system or handle her own problems. Both avenues lead to stress and strife in the household; I have learned this the hard way.

So, before you can tackle your home and family organization system, take some time to assess everyone's personality traits and figure out the pros and cons of each tendency. The goal here is not to judge each other as worthy or wanting but to figure out a way for everyone to be happy and to minimize the daily stress of living. If I can find a system that helps Isabelle find her shoes easily and does not require my time or energy, that is a win. And it doesn't matter if said shoes are all lined up on the floor of her room and not in neatly labeled bins. It matters that she gets to class on time without being stressed or calling me to come help her.

Thus, the key here is to put yourself into someone else's shoes (pun intended). It is way too easy to put your expectations and assumptions out there, but much more difficult to see that your opinions do not hold value with people who see the world differently. For example, it seems obvious that the family would love to have the playroom nicely organized with all the like toys put together in nice little baggies. This is what my husband thought when we designated a play area in our home and set out to put the kids' toys away. He thought it was obvious that all the Polly Pocket toys should be together, separated from the Littlest Pet Shop. However, the girls liked to comingle the toys because Polly Pocket loved to go down the slide in the Littlest Pet Shop. Therefore, everything was always jumbled. My collector husband wanted the pieces together because, of course, these toys might be worth something someday, but not if the sets were missing crucial pieces. The kids, though, had creative minds that saw beyond the boundaries of being "mint in box." (Of course, our daughters won out; they have my husband wrapped around their little fingers.) So, take it from me, using the time now to figure out how everyone sees the world is going to help you establish a nice base of **patience** — which is the most essential tool in your upcoming organizational journey.

It's pretty easy to figure out everyone's overall organizational personality. There are numerous quizzes on the internet that can help you, but from my experience there are a handful of options. Each person might cross over into different categories, of course, but he or she will have a dominant organizational personality. Obviously, this is a little bit simplistic, but it is a place to start.

Organized to the T: the Minimalist
This person tends to be more than a little OCD on clutter. It is more important to have everything put away and in its place. In fact, you probably feel anxiety if all the dirty dishes are not in the dishwasher or cleaned immediately and put away. Your dream house is minimalist with clean lines and no clutter. Other people might see your space as sterile. If your kids bring home art projects, they are admired and put away or trashed. (No judgment, I have been known to do this. Once, in the middle of a house move, the kids went to an amazing Vacation Bible School and came home with epic crafts. I literally eyeballed them and put them immediately into a contractor grade black trash bag—not my best mother moment admittedly.) You can have the nature/nurture debate all you want, but people who grow up in small spaces with tidy moms might have the fear of too much stuff. So, you also probably have some form of claustrophobia and feel closed in by a house with too many items. Ideally you live alone.

Wishes to be Organized but Can't Manage to do so: the Procrastinator
This person desires to have a fantastic organizational system. In fact, you pore over closet systems and planners. You spend money on them but are paralyzed when it comes time to use them or put them into ac-

tion. You yearn for the peace and stress relief that comes from knowing where everything is, but you just can't create the system or manage to keep up the system that someone makes for you. Your home probably has a mash up of sentimental items along with a big pile of junk mail that just keeps growing on the kitchen counter. You might even exist somewhere on the ADHD spectrum. Others might perceive you as a hoarder because you cannot throw away items—mainly because you haven't found the time yet to go through them. When not medicated, things fall apart. Important deeds or school papers get lost, you miss appointments, and you end up buying another black sweater to add to the ten black sweaters that you already own. You need me. I don't understand you, but I feel you and I think I can help. Your biggest challenge is learning to live with people like me.

Has high expectations that must be upheld at all costs: the Perfectionist

This person wants to be organized but will not attempt the job unless it can be accomplished fully and completely. Organization is an ALL OR NOTHING prospect. For example, in the process of cleaning out the kitchen junk drawer, the perfectionist will take everything out and clean the drawer and every little item completely. The drawer will be fully taken apart and cleaned in every nook and cranny. The job is not done until it is done perfectly with each item facing the right direction and fitting correctly. Because it is difficult to be perfect, these tasks can defeat the perfectionist personality. This striving for perfection will often keep a person from even tackling a job since there would not be enough time or energy to fully accomplish the task. It is hard for these individuals to recognize that done is better than perfect.

Loves collections and keepsakes: the Sentimental Soul

When I'm at a dinner party I sometimes like to throw out the conversation starter question, "Do you have any collections at your house?" I have a friend who likes frogs, so everyone in her life brings her frog items, from keychains to paperweights. Another couple I know collects a refrigerator magnet from every vacation so that they can see all their travels each morning when they grab creamer for their coffee before heading off to work. If I encounter people who truly don't see themselves as collectors of anything, a little prodding will reveal something that they own too much of—like beauty supplies, books, or sports equipment. And most of us own sentimental items like scrapbooks, photographs, children's artwork, and family heirlooms. Some people can whittle down sentimental items without too much trauma. However, others are really attached to objects and invoke them with sentimental feelings. If this describes someone you know, don't worry; I have some ideas on how to keep family traditions alive and still maintain order in your home.

Doesn't see the Need for Organization: the Free Spirit
You pride yourself on hanging out, finding new experiences, and learning from life. You don't need to organize yourself or your family because you are out living the dream and don't have to worry about little details like laundry or what's for dinner tonight. You don't need this book—keep doing what you are doing. If I win the Powerball lottery, maybe I can be this person! (Who am I kidding? I am hardwired to be a "momager"—mom manager. My kids often call me Kris Jenner, and I don't think that is a compliment.) The free spirit personality is independent of money—you are footloose and fancy free and a rare bird that should spread his or her wings. We can all admire you from afar (while we fold laundry and buy toilet paper and household cleaning products).

Has an organization system but it needs tweaking: the Organizational Student
If you picked up this book, there is a good chance that you fit into this category and live with some of the other personalities listed here. You have a system that worked when you lived alone and you can manage to get your lunch packed, your taxes done, and your towel hung up in the bathroom. However, things break down when others join your household, and you must keep your system going while co-existing with others' stuff. It's not easy. I feel your pain. You float from sys-

tem to system, organizational book to organizational book. You try baskets from Target, clear canisters from the Container Store, fancy label makers and chalkboard paint. But you are hampered by the people who live with you and refuse to buy into your system. They thwart you and sometimes ridicule you. Some days it feels like war. Some days you wave a white flag of surrender. Some days you decide to go on strike and drink two glasses of wine at book club. But you keep coming back for more. You must love these people and you must figure out how to make things work and keep your sanity. I'm here for you. Let's do it together.

Like I said, you probably ebb and flow between a couple of these organizational personalities. In fact, my daughter Isabelle pointed out that her ADHD makes her mostly a procrastinator. However, when she takes ADHD medications during the school year, she moves over to perfectionism. Your family members probably cannot be pigeonholed exclusively either. And just to complicate things, your home will go through different phases of life while you switch these personalities. When your children are young, you will have toys and an active play life to add to the mix. When you are working hard, you will be too tired to pick up stuff, let alone clean the house. When you are empty nesting, you think you will have more time, but you will be dealing with adult children boomeranging back to the nest, more travel and/or a busier work and social life. Give yourself permission now to realize that life situations can turn us all into "organizational students." While you might tend to be a minimalist, procrastinator, sentimental soul or free spirit, life's curveballs can throw all home order out the window. It's okay. We all have been there or will be there. If depression, death, illness, or general busy-ness comes into your life, take some deep breaths. Clutter can get a foothold in your life and chaos can reign temporarily. The good thing about being an organizational student is that you can get back on track. Stick with me and we will do it together.

In the meantime, take a moment to read these different personality perspectives to see if they sound like anyone you know:

HERE'S THE SITUATION:
One spouse is an artist and creates amazing art pieces. Ther other spouse is frustrated by the clutter in the artist's workspace.

Spouse Perspective:
I can't stand seeing craft supplies strewn all over our family room. I'd like to work on my hobby too, but I can't with all this stuff everywhere. It is driving me crazy!"

Artist Perspective:
Having to stay organized and keep from being messy stifles the creative process for me and people like me. I actually want everything organized and I see benefit in it, but I can't hinder my creative mode by putting everything back where it goes or cleaning up all the small messes as I go. I get distracted easily and I don't want to lose my concentration on what I am doing. I get excited about creating and I want to stay on that streak or else I won't accomplish as much or be as creative as I could be. I see people do this with baking or cooking where the kitchen looks like a tornado went through when they are done. I understand them. This doesn't mean that I don't want to live in an organized environment. I want things clean and put away. However, that must be done when I'm in a different mindset, when my purpose is to clean up and organize and not to create. I admit that this mindset doesn't come around that often because I look at my media and I want to create. It's probably a lack of discipline but the tidiness seems trivial to the potential of creating great things.

HERE'S THE SITUATION:
You want your child with ADHD to pick up her messy room and manage to get to school without you having to wake her up in the morning. Your child also wants her room clean and to make it to school on time.

Parent perspective:
I don't know why she can't get it together. I just want to pull my hair out. Her inability to meet basic deadlines is creating a lot of anxiety for me.

ADHD perspective:
You think you have anxiety? Ha! You don't know anxiety. Try living in a world where everyone else is managing to get things done but you have no idea how they are doing it. I don't know how people manage to get ready in the morning so easily. I don't know how people clean their rooms all at once. I don't know how people cook meals and get all the dishes cleaned and put away. I don't know where I put my keys, my drivers' license, and my favorite pair of shoes. I really try hard, but I don't know how to keep my mind from wandering. It's like I'm living in a pinball machine and every bell and whistle takes me in a different direction. Some days I just don't want to get out of bed because I know I'm going to fail.

HERE'S THE SITUATION:
Your husband is complaining that you never finish any tasks. You start things all the time but can't ever reach completion because you want everything to be perfect.

Husband perspective:
My wife is a fantastic person, but she has very high expectations for all of us in the family. In the meantime, she starts projects but never finishes them. I don't think she even notices that we are the ones going behind her and actually getting things done.

Perfectionist perspective:
I was never good enough for my mother. Every time I tried to do something to please her, my mother found something wrong with me. I remember in seventh grade I spent several weeks in art class sketching out her favorite bench in our community garden. When I proudly presented it to her, she told me it was nice but that I had to work on my shading better. I know that I am sometimes hard on my children, and I really try to curb that behavior so that I don't end up damaging their self-esteem. However, I cannot help it—all I can see are the areas that could be better, and I think sometimes that I am helping my family by pointing out ways they can improve. Therapy is helping me notice these tendencies, and I work hard to be loving and not complaining. However, I struggle with my own sense of worth and have difficulty starting new things because I know that I will fail. When I do start things, I prefer that someone else finishes the tasks for me so that I know that things will get done in the best way possible.

Some of these scenarios might remind you of yourself or someone you know. It's these types of interchanges that create strife in the household and put you at odds with other family members. Our goal throughout this book is to come to some understanding of each other and to find ways to coexist harmoniously in the home.

CHAPTER ONE CHEAT SHEET

Organizational Personalities and Their Key Attributes:

The Minimalist

- Clean, stark home
- Less is more: no clutter
- Possibly exhibits obsessive-compulsive traits

The Procrastinator

- Indecisive
- Easily distracted
- Has difficulty keeping a routine
- Possibly exhibits ADHD traits

The Perfectionist

- Takes too long when performing small tasks
- Unable to fully complete tasks to personal satisfaction
- Possibly exhibits some depression over organization

The Sentimental Soul

- Hesitant to make decisions about objects
- Infuses objects with emotion
- Likes to create collections
- Likes to give meaningful gifts to others
- Possibly has poor memory traits and keeps items for reminders

The Free Spirit
- Doesn't care about routines or organizational systems
- Prefers to experience life rather than do mundane tasks
- Encourages others to live life rather than work on minutia
- Possibly more focused on self rather than group needs

The Organizational Student
- Constantly seeks ways to improve routines and organizational systems
- Tries to help others get organized
- Focused on group goals and visions
- Possibly annoying to all the other organizational personalities

(2)

A WORD OR TWO ABOUT HOARDING AND COLLECTING

The A&E television show *Hoarders* made us all aware of the psychological disorder of hoarding; yet we still throw around that word too often. I even put the word "hoarder" in the subtitle of this book because I know that organized people often see sentimental collectors as hoarders. Some people who live in beautifully curated, stark homes can't conceive of a home lovingly peppered with artwork by children and Precious Moments statuary. Thus, they might label the next-door neighbors as hoarders when really the neighbors just enjoy a different home aesthetic.

However, it is important to note that compulsive hoarding is a classified mental disorder. According to the American Psychiatric Association, it is an official mental health diagnosis that is often present with other mental conditions like depression and anxiety. Individuals with this diagnosis have difficulty in parting with items and feel compelled to "save" the objects, often at the detriment of living conditions. The resulting clutter can create unhygienic spaces that are often unsafe due to the number of items and inability to clean the space. Hoarding occurs equally in men and women and affects about 2.6% of the population.

The term "hoarder" thus has negative connotations and conjures up images of filthy homes populated by too many pets. People with this mental condition differ, though, from collectors who purposely acquire items and attempt to display or categorize them in their home. While I may have jokingly referred to my husband as a hoarder; he is, more accurately, a collector and fits into the role of a sentimental soul. When Todd was at the hospital fighting to breathe and live with COVID, we knew he had turned the corner when he sent the family thread this text, "I'm doing better. Don't sell all my stuff."

All kidding aside, hoarding is not a laughing matter and if you or someone you live with falls into the realm of compulsive hoarding, then you should seek the services of mental health professionals who can develop a treatment plan that includes counseling and other services designed to help individuals deal with this mental condition. Simply employing organizational tips like the ones in this book will not help you. This situation requires professional mental health assistance.

Since collectors are often mislabeled as hoarders, they often get a bad rap. I'll admit that I have been concerned about the amount of stuff that my husband collects. We are lucky in the fact that he has a storage area separate from our home where he can warehouse and categorize his items. I don't understand the need to acquire objects; personally, I prefer to spend money on experiences like eating at a restaurant or going to a concert. Many of our fights have stemmed from his desire to own a lot of stuff and my desire to have a beautiful home free of clutter.

You may be in a similar situation where you or someone in your family has collections that have some personal meaning, like memorabilia from the 1980s, angel statues or t-shirts from every 5K race for the past

10 years. These collections could be literally anything and you might find them stupid or useless. However, to your family members, that collection contains a lot of emotions. That collection might be wrapped up in family sentiment or simply represent a lot of good memories.

What I have learned from being married to a collector is that owning objects satisfies a need in Todd that I do not have. If you have ever read the book, *The Five Love Languages* by Gary Chapman, then you know that one of the love languages is gift-giving. My husband is an excellent gift giver. He pays attention to what people like and if he sees something that reminds him of a friend or family member, he buys that item immediately so he can give it to that person. Much of the stuff we own is kept by my husband "just in case" someone might need that item in the future. For example, he has made us keep all our Halloween costumes labeled in plastic tubs in case we need to use them again or so others can borrow them from us. I must admit, all our daughters have rummaged through the tubs and utilized these costumes, and we have had friends and neighbors come over to borrow last-minute outfits. While I would love to donate all these costumes since I don't think I'll be Cleopatra or Wonder Woman again anytime soon, it is important to Todd to have these costumes on hand to help meet the needs of other people.

Similarly, Todd keeps a plethora of dishware, furniture, and camping gear on hand so that the kids can borrow or take what they need. Since our children are just now getting into homes of their own and have their own storage areas, we are finally at the point where Todd can let some things go.

In any relationship it is important to know where each party is coming from. We both have the goal of having a nice home with less clutter. Where we diverge is in our solutions. I would simply give away or sell all extra items. My husband wants to organize and store extra items. What is important here is that THE GOAL IS THE SAME! This is something to keep in mind as we go forward on this journey to organize our lives and homes and keep everyone happy.

In an article in the *Huffington Post*, author Caroline Bologna outlined several reasons why people create collections: for nostalgia reasons, for a sense of accomplishment or power, for a sense of hope for the future, for feelings of comfort and control, for self-expression, for creating connections with others and for investment purposes ("Why Millennials Are So Into Collecting Things"). Through research with different experts, Bologna concluded that the global COVID pandemic caused a resurgence in collecting as people were more housebound and sought comfort and enjoyment through collections. When the outside world is chaotic or alarming, collections can provide us with purpose and distraction. Also, completing collections can provide people with a sense of personal accomplishment that might be lacking in other areas of their lives. For some collectors, it is the thrill of the chase of finding the objects necessary to complete the collection. For others, the collection has a monetary value or, at least, a hopeful high value in the future.

My husband is a mix of several of these categories; stuff just makes him happy. However, he is realistic about future values. His coins will increase in value but everything else is subject to current trends and fashions. Beanie Babies are a great lesson in being realistic about collection values. In the 1990s, people went crazy over these cute stuffed animals and the Ty company who created the toys, drove up the frenzy by making limited quantities. People really thought that they were building future value by tracking down different Beanie Babies. Some people said it was how they were investing in their retirement or in their kids' college educations. You probably know the rest of the story—the market for Beanie Babies went bust and now you can't even give the cute little things away, let alone make any money from them.

If the impetus for collecting is nostalgia and you don't mind knowing that you might be buying something that will not increase or even just hold its value, then there is no delusion issue. However, if your collector really thinks that those items that he or she has hit upon will be the next big thing and if this collection is taking over your home and costing you a lot of money upfront, then you may need to address these concerns. Also, if the collecting really crosses over to a compulsive shopping or buying disorder, then you will need to seek some mental health assistance.

Compulsive shopping hits about 3-6 percent of the population and sometimes happens at different stages of life, showing that this behavior is more a reaction to some other stressors. Experts say that 80 percent of compulsive shoppers are women, but that those numbers are changing in the digital era. A good mental health professional will be able to delve better into the reasons behind this type of compulsion and provide strategies to help alleviate the situation. Some characteristics of compulsive shopping include impulsive purchasing, preoccupation with shopping, constant acquisition of unneeded items and financial difficulties from overspending. Those who shop compulsively will also experience emotional turmoil, starting with a shopper's high or euphoria at buying stuff and bottoming out with guilt and remorse. Thus, compulsive shoppers will often have relationship difficulty as their friends and family will not understand their impulsive purchasing and try to curb the behavior. Most experts agree that the best way to help compulsive shopping is to seek out group therapy and cognitive behavior therapy.

Take time to talk to the collectors in your household and listen to the reasons they have for creating collections and obtaining stuff. If there are no health risks or mental health barriers, then find a way to communicate with the collectors in your life so that you can both be happy in your home. In Chapter 7, I will address ideas on how to contain and organize collections so that everyone can be happy in your shared space.

You might be asking yourself,

Why are collectors so into stuff?

Here are several reasons why people collect things:

1. **Nostalgia**

    A lot of collectors like to find things from childhood or things that remind them of the past. My husband loves Star Wars and collects the original, late 1970s action figures because they remind him of the hours of fun that he had playing with his brother. Also, for many collectors, adulthood frees up more discretionary funds so they can afford all the toys that they couldn't get as children. Since toys are often tied to good memories, these are a popular collecting category. You might also collect dishware that you admired at your great aunt's house as child or historic memorabilia from a specific region or event.

2. **Accomplishment**

    Collectors often like to complete things or finish a huge collection. Finding every Dr. Seuss book might be a fun scavenger hunt for you and your family and when you are able to check off the box on the last title, you will all feel a great sense of accomplishment. This can make you feel powerful and confident about an achievement and further fuel the desire to pursue collections.

3. **Hope for the Future**

    In the 15th and 16th centuries, many European countries saw the tradition of dowry chests, or hope chests, start to come into eminence. Colonial settlers brought this tradition to the United States in the 18th century when sturdy wooden boxes were made to house all the dowry items for an unmarried woman. Called "hope chests," these containers held items made and collected by the woman and her other female relatives, like linens, quilts, wedding clothing, dishes, and other important household items.

The chest and its contents represented the hope for marriage, thereby ensuring the future for the single woman. Since modern women do not need marriage to thrive and survive, this practice has largely died out. However, people still collect items out of hope, like dishware for an anticipated new home or decorations for future holidays. Pleasure is gained from these collections because they represent a hope for bigger and better things in the future.

4 Comfort and Control

When the rest of your life is chaotic and uncertain, collections can provide a sense of security. You might not be able to control external factors like your job schedule, your work assignments, your general health, your living conditions, and so on—but you can control the items you choose to collect and keep with you. These items can provide a sense of comfort since they are tangible items that you are choosing to keep, and it is an aspect of life that you are able to control. I once rented an apartment to a gentleman named Bill who was an alcoholic and who had difficulty keeping a steady job and maintaining a healthy lifestyle. He lived in a small studio apartment with just a few pieces of furniture but a large collection of angel statuary, numbering in the hundreds. When I ultimately had to evict him for nonpayment of rent, my office staff had to store all of Bill's belongings for 30 days. Bill was not concerned about his clothing, household goods or personal papers, but he really wanted to regain control over his angels. He told me that he collected the angels over the years and felt that having them in his home provided him with some love and protection. Bill could not control much in his life, but the angels were something he could collect to provide personal comfort.

5 Self-expression

Many people choose to collect things that are an outward representation of self-expression. For example, my friends who collect travel magnets for their refrigerator are not only enjoying those memories, but they are also projecting to their visitors the fact that they identify as world travelers. People who collect vintage clothing are showing the world that they identify as someone with a cool vintage vibe. And those who collect all the latest limited releases of tennis shoes are showing their desire to be on trend and in the know. Jay Leno is famous for his high-end collection of vintage automobiles. He is showing the world that he is not just defined as a great comedian and host but is also a cool gearhead.

6 Connections with Others

Even before the advent of the internet, collectors sought each other out in different niche audiences. For decades, collectors have gone to gun shows, coin shows, teddy bear conventions and cocktail stir stick conferences. Collectors have also sought each other out in newsletters, magazines, and bulletin boards. The internet has made this desire to connect even easier, with apps, Facebook groups, online blogs, and other platforms. Now collectors can watch videos on YouTube about their favorite collections and discuss the different aspects of their belongings with people from around the world. When my husband comes across another coin collector at a cocktail party or other event, he is happy to discuss the various aspects of his large cent collection with someone who understands and supports his collection.

7 Investment Purposes

Not all collections go up in value; in fact, most collections probably lose money over time. If you have ever watched *Antiques Roadshow* on PBS or YouTube, then you know that some items will peak in value on the filming date and then lose value ten years later when trends change, or the market is saturated with too many similar items. When eBay first premiered in the 1990s, collectors were finally able to find their items more easily than hunting store after store. Of course, this affected the price of items. For example, people in California who sought out early American antiques saw that they could find these items cheaper online from East coast suppliers than in their local shops. The use of eBay helped fuel the Beanie Babies madness since it became a platform for people to find rare animals that they could not find in their local stores. Some savvy collectors are choosing to take entrepreneurial risks to obtain items that they think will become more valuable in the future. And some items that have traditionally gained in value include coins, classic cars, fine art, vintage wines, stamps, watches, sports cards, and celebrity memorabilia.

Because collectors enjoy stuff so much, they will have **specific concerns** about their collections when it comes time to organize the home. Here are some things that they want you to know before you take on the task of reorganizing their belongings:

- **Collectors like their stuff.** Like, a lot. So don't throw it out without asking them. And don't pack it all up and put it somewhere where they will never find the items. In fact, they prefer it if you admire the stuff, but don't touch it or rearrange it. Instead, talk to them about their collections. Let them know that you respect their collections and that you just want to work together to find options of how to keep the house organized and keep all their stuff.

- **Collectors want to have ways to display their amazing collections.** They are open to ideas about acquiring display shelves, cabinetry, and shadow boxes. Collectors dream of having lighted areas where everything is in one place, looking magnificent. They know that their collectibles take up a lot of space and that nice display areas might have to wait until a child moves away from home or you acquire a bigger place to live. The collectors are in this for the long run, so they will be patient about finalizing their collection with a fantastic public display.

- **Collectors would like to have ample table space with good lighting** where they can peruse their collection, looking at dates on coins, searching for identifying marks and cataloguing everything into a database. They would prefer that this space is an area that doesn't have to be cleaned up at the end of every day but can be a "work in progress" area for a few days or weeks. While you cannot let collectors take over important areas like your kitchen table and the family living room, think about places that can be carved out for them, like an unused basement room or an outdoor shed area.

- **Collectors sometimes fear that people will steal their items,** so they want a safe area to keep items when they are not on display, like a locked cabinet or an area that is not easily accessible to thieves. Small items, like jewelry, watches, coins, and stamps are particularly easy for people to take without someone noticing. Thus, collectors will often seek out safes or locked cabinets that can keep their precious items safe.

- **Collectors like to have a plethora of boxes, containers, and cubbies** to store items while they are being acquired or packed. They like to choose their own items. I once tried to help my husband by acquiring several plastic containers. I thought opaque ones were best to keep out sunlight, but he wanted clear ones so he could see immediately what he had in the container. Let collectors think about the best types of organization for their collections. You can help them by measuring items and finding containers for a reasonable price.

- **Collectors like to have an avenue to sell or liquidate items that no longer fit into the collection.** They would like to find another like-minded collector who appreciates the item. Furthermore, they would like to use the monetary proceeds to purchase another item for their overall collection instead of having the monies just go into the general family fund. In Chapter 10, I will discuss several ways you can help your collector in selling items.

Your family members who collect things are not your enemies. They just have deep, emotional attachments to items. This can sometimes be hard to understand. Certainly, you will need to navigate the issue with them since collections cannot take over the entire family home and your collectors need to respect your space as well. I will discuss this aspect further in Chapter Seven.

CHAPTER TWO CHEAT SHEET

Collectors are NOT Hoarders.

Hoarding is a specific mental disorder that requires professional intervention.

Why do People Collect Things?
- Nostalgia
- Accomplishment
- Hope for the future
- Comfort and control
- Self-expression
- Connections with others
- Investment purposes

Collectors are Concerned About:
- Keeping their stuff
- Having people admire their stuff
- Having people respect their stuff
- Having ways to display their collections
- Having a table or room to work on their collections
- Keeping their items safe from theft or removal
- Having the right types of containers to hold their items
- Liquidating items to other worthy collectors

(3)

A WORD OR TWO ABOUT ADHD, DEFIANCE AND PROCRASTINATION

ADHD, or Attention-deficit/hyperactivity disorder, is a common mental health condition that is usually diagnosed in childhood but can affect people through adulthood. Scientists are unsure of why some people exhibit ADHD symptoms and whether it is caused by genetic, physical, or social conditions. The main markers of ADHD are inattention, hyperactivity, and impulsivity. People with ADHD may exhibit one or all of these conditions. ADHD is usually diagnosed by mental health specialists or physicians. There is no single test for this disorder so if you are concerned that someone in your family has ADHD, seek more information from your medical provider who can get you in touch with a licensed professional who can provide diagnosis and treatment assistance.

In addition, there are also a lot of great resources on the internet. My family members particularly like the approach by Kelly Baums, an ADHD coach who posts informative and entertaining videos on her TikTok channel. Kelly often delves into topics like how to know if you have ADHD, how to get ADHD resources and strategies for dealing with ADHD. We also found a few great private Facebook groups that provide great information and support. One you might check out is *How to Align Your Ducks—ADHD-friendly Home Organization & Decluttering* moderated by Ilona Torniainen. Her private group provides a safe forum where you can get some great tips and tricks to deal with ADHD organizational issues. If your loved one is really struggling, hiring an ADHD life coach might be a great option for getting him or her the emotional support and life hacks needed to get on track and be more productive.

When it comes to life organization, individuals with ADHD often struggle to maintain systems, develop routines, and stay on task. In fact, regular life is harder for those with ADHD. While they are wildly creative, curious, and prone towards risk-taking and impulsiveness, ADHD folks struggle to stay on task and complete basic activities of daily living. In fact, studies show that people with ADHD can develop organizational strategies but might have trouble using those strategies on a regular, ongoing basis. In a study completed in 2020, researchers Durand, Arbone and Wharton postulated that "reduced organizational skills in adults with ADHD are due to deficits in persistence, not in strategies."

So, while ADHD people are often attracted to high-risk careers and curious about everything, they can struggle to keep a steady, daily routine. A cursory search of Amazon or your library shelves will show you a plethora of titles dedicated to ADHD. There are books to assist you with raising children, finding a job, keeping a job, strengthening your marriage, dealing with anxiety, staying on task, taking charge of your life, and so on. Since ADHD impacts so many important relationships and mental health concerns, it only makes sense that it will have a profound impact on the way you see your life schedules and organizational systems.

For example, my daughter and I both have a different style of living. I remember vividly being in the car when she was in ninth grade and berating her for not being better organized. She was losing school papers, constantly daydreaming and incapable of getting ready for school on time in the morning. It was a low point of parenting; I even called her out as simply being defiant and reduced her to tears. Shortly thereafter, a good counselor referred my daughter for ADHD testing, and we found out that she was off the chart in terms of attention deficit, which, in hindsight, made a lot of sense. Every day, for Isabelle and me, the goal was the same: for her to be able to find her stuff in her room and get places on time. However, her ADHD was paralyzing her; she could not find the first step in the process of getting organized. Finding ways to help Isabelle de-clutter had to be more detail oriented. Because she could not find the individual steps, I had to make her a clear, easy to follow outline. While I could simply tell my older daughters to put away their clean, laundered clothing, I had to put Isabelle's items in different baskets so she could more easily locate items. If a shirt was buried under 20 other items, it simply did not exist for her and caused all-out panic. Instead, we had to get creative and restructure her closet with all open bins and no drawers.

Again, Isabelle and I SHARED THE SAME GOAL. Where problems arose were in our solutions. It seemed obvious to me that she should simply put things away. After all, this worked for me, my husband and our other two daughters. I could not conceive of any other solution. For Isabelle, however, my system simply made no sense to her. Why would she put everything away? She needed to see her options. If things were put away, they were hidden and might as well be nonexistent. Not only did she need more assistance from me upfront, but she also needed me to listen to her and understand that my life organization methods were not going to work for her.

People with ADHD often have difficulty with executive function which is a group of complex mental processes and cognitive abilities that control skills needed to complete goals. Like people with dementia, your ADHD people will have problems with remembering things, staying on track, maintaining focus, and managing time limits. Executive dysfunction will impact people in other ways too, since it can cause them to lose confidence, to not meet important goals and to avoid trying new things. So, this means that in addition to household organization, your ADHD family members might also need help with things you consider to be simple activities of daily living. People with ADHD are particularly susceptible to task shifting issues. When distractions occur, they will leap from task to task, thinking they are multitasking, but, in reality, they are floundering—frittering away the day in shifting among a myriad of interruptions. In further chapters, I will discuss ways to help create cheat sheets, reminders and plans to help ADHDers map out their daily and weekly tasks.

In summary, when you are working with your family members to get organized and stay on track, not only are you dealing with varying opinions on what stuff should be kept, but you are also dealing with people who see the world differently. My husband's love language of gifting meant he wanted to store more stuff. And my daughter's ADHD kept her from following my organizational system for the family. Within your own family you are probably dealing with any or all of these types of situations:

- People who don't understand your system of organization.
- People who thwart your system of organization.
- People who don't care about your system of organization.
- People who want you to just take a chill pill already.

My youngest daughter wanted to get organized. Isabelle was performing poorly in school and knew she was floundering. She compared herself to her older sisters who were able to follow along with the household schedule and routine that we had in place. Thus, she was willing to accept help. **However, you might have family members who are just simply defiant.** They rebel against the order that you try to impose. This can be very difficult and emotionally draining. We all know people who struggle with their teenagers' constant excuses and backtalk. You might even be that someone. These parents are often tempted to simply perform tasks FOR the defiant teens, like putting alerts on their telephones for important meetings and pulling out their softball uniforms for laundering from their duffle bags. But what this is NOT doing is preparing teens for an adult life away from the home. I get it—it takes longer to explain to your children how and why to do something than to simply perform the task yourself. In the case of keeping a calendar, the parent can put in those alerts while watching Netflix, instead of arguing with the kids about the need to keep a calendar and be accountable to others. And in the case of stinky uniforms, it is so much easier to grab the bags, empty them, and launder as quick as possible, rather than deal with the fallout from cranky daughters when it is game time, and the uniforms aren't ready. However, if you fall into this category too often, then you may soon be coping with children who have no life organization skills and who underperform in school.

As you can see, organizing your life and home is an emotional journey. We have already established that it requires dealing with various personalities and maybe even a mental condition in the mix. Outright opposition from the people you are trying to help is a roadblock that may seem unsurmountable. However, delve in a little further. Does the rebellion stem from another source?

Here are some reasons you might be encountering opposition:

1 **Bad timing:**

   Nobody wants to drop everything they are doing to help you get things in order. I have been accused of this a time or two. I would look around the house and perceive that my children were all just sitting around, so of course it seemed like the best time for us to tackle their cluttered, messy closets. But my kids were just hanging around because that is what they wanted to do at that time. I learned that giving advance notice was the best way to gain buy-in to my project. Also, I started instituting clean out closet days in the summer BEFORE we embarked on back-to-school shopping, which was a much anticipated, fun day for my daughters. We would clean out the closets and make lists of what clothing items the kids needed for the upcoming year. Scheduling organization sessions with your family accords them the respect they deserve and ensures a better rate of success than surprise clean-outs.

2   **Not knowing the first step:**

Some people are paralyzed with fear about starting something new. If you are not well versed in organization, then you might not even know where to begin. So just telling someone to clear out and organize the closet might be met with resistance, simply because she or he is clueless. That is why it is important that you, as the organized one, assist in the process. When I asked my kids to clean their closets, I participated in the process by coming in with donate boxes and trash bags and walking them through the process. I did not do the task for them once they were old enough to tackle the project, but I would at least get them started and check on them periodically.

3   **Expecting too much:**

Are you imposing organization in an area that your people do not see as important? For example, do you want to color code everything in the garage when it is already organized? Is your husband perfectly happy with the state of his man cave and does he prefer that you not organize the room? Are your kids happy with all their stuffed animals in a jumble on their shelves? Because honestly, if it is not your space, why even get involved unless it is unsafe or unsanitary? This might be an example of your own sense of perfection or anxiety coming through. Sometimes the status quo is perfectly acceptable. Make sure to step back and see if your requests are unreasonable or out of the range of normalcy.

4 **Not seeing the task as important:**

Often my family thinks the house looks just fine. However, I know we are having new people over to visit who will want to take a tour and see the rest of the home. Thus, I ask the kids to assist in a major pick-up, including making their beds and stashing all the clutter somewhere it cannot be seen. I have the vision of a perfect, beautiful home, but my kids think everything looks just fine. After all, their friends come over all the time and no one worries about an unmade bed. So, our visions are just not in tune with each other. In fact, to highlight the discrepancy, my kids have made me watch a YouTube video by comedian Chris Fleming called "Company is Coming!" where Chris acts out a scene as a crazy housewife, Gayle Water-Waters, who is trying to galvanize her family into getting the house ready for company. A couple of her lines that my kids still quote back to me when they think I need to calm the F down include: "I want this place looking like Disney on Ice in one minute!" and "There cannot be any signs of living in this house!" On one level, they are right; why should I worry about what someone thinks of us by viewing our home? In fact, I don't have to offer any house tours! But on another level, my family knows it is important to me to have an orderly home and sometimes having company is the impetus we use to get things picked up.

5 **Not understanding your system:**

ome of my family members do not understand my system of getting things done. For example, they do not see the utility in making a daily list. In fact, planning things out the night before stresses them out. Where I find it empowering to plan out my clothing and tasks for the next day, a couple of my children are made anxious by that process. They would rather spend the evening listening to music, hanging out with a friend, or vegging out in front of the television. Preparing for the next day just gets them down. My system does not work for them. This is where I need to back off on imposing my ideas but instead help them in developing a system that achieves the same goal that we all share — which is to get things done and be productive members of society.

Therefore, what an organized person might perceive as laziness or defiance is often more nuanced. There are discrepancies in our personalities, in our circumstances and in our life outlooks that make this issue more difficult. Just because we all live in the same house does not mean we all see the world the same, even if you have raised some of these people from birth. This is hard for parents to realize. You understand the organizational chaos when you are a group of roommates or college students coming from different backgrounds and sharing a common space. That is when you truly learn to navigate your threshold for clutter and chaos. However, we are harder on the people we love, and we expect each child to be our mini-me—seeing the world the same and doing things the same. Nothing could be further from the truth.

Procrastination is another whole category that organized persons will come up against. Procrastination is when a person puts off a task until a later time or even past a deadline. It is not a mental health disorder, but procrastination can cause people mental distress or anguish and be accompanied with depression and anxiety. Of course, we all procrastinate at one time or another; however, for some people this will impede relationships, careers, and life events. In an interview with the American Psychological Association, Joseph Ferrari, PhD, and professor of psychology, related that according to his research, 20 percent of the American population are chronic procrastinators. And some experts postulate that this number will rise with the exponential growth of social media, streaming and other technological aspects at our disposal.

It can be very difficult for us organizers to deal with people who procrastinate. From my research, scientists do not know if procrastination is genetic or runs in families or is even something that is a specific personality or a mental block. Many experts even postulate that procrastination is a deliberate decision to avoid complicated or distressing issues. Dr. Joseph Ferrari postulates in his book, *Still Procrastinating: The No Regrets Guide to Getting it Done*, that procrastination is a learned bad habit that can only be changed with hard work, over time. Honestly, it does not matter whether you perceive procrastination as real or made up, your people believe in it, own it, and identify with it—therefore you need to deal with it.

Here are some common procrastinator outlooks that you might recognize in yourself and members of your family:

1   I can do it tomorrow.

Mark Twain famously quipped, "Never put off till tomorrow what may be done day after tomorrow just as well." Many people think that procrastinators simply put off tasks for a later time in favor of doing easier or more fun projects. Of course, this is something we all do. If I must make a difficult decision or phone call, sometimes I will rearrange the spice cabinet, dust all the woodwork or put away laundry, simply because I am avoiding the inevitable sucky task. Most experts agree that the simple aspect of time management is not what really impedes people, but rather procrastination is a reaction to the negative feelings of anxiety or boredom. This is when you simply pull out the calendar and ask your procrastinator, "What time works tomorrow?" Get it on a list to check off and a calendar alert to capture his or her fleeting attention span.

2   I work better under pressure.

The procrastinators in my life actually believe this sentiment. However, academic research shows that this adage does not hold true. In 2001, psychologist Dr. Joseph Ferrari worked with university students to study procrastination and see if procrastinators performed better under pressure. His results revealed that people who waited until the deadline made more errors, did not finish tasks, and performed poorly compared to non-procrastinators.

Interestingly, the same procrastinators who performed badly vocalized that they thought they did as well as, if not better than, people who did not procrastinate. What this tells us organizers is that we will have to deal with some delusion when it comes to these deadline-challenged members of the family. My recommendation is to simply keep gently stating the obvious, "That is not true," until they begin to see the error of their ways. Alternatively, you can point out that while the procrastinator works well under pressure, you do not, so a clean-up session needs to be scheduled.

3   **Someone else will do the task.**

In my home, I get irritated because people will leave dirty dishes around the house and not carry them to the dishwasher. As soon as I see the dishes, I pick them up and do the task. My husband, a procrastinator, will say "I was going to do it later." It is a timing issue and a distraction issue for him. He does not multitask, so even though he got up to go to the bathroom and to let the dog outside, he did not think about carrying his bowl to the dishwasher along the way. And in the meantime, the dish always magically disappears because his wife comes along and performs that task. So, of course, why would he go out of his way to put the bowl away? If this situation sounds familiar to you, there are a couple options here that you need to consider. If it doesn't bother you to be the official picker-upper, then just do the task and don't complain about it. However, if you don't have the time or the issue really gets under your skin, then discuss the matter. You will need to NOT do the task and let the other person start to realize that there is no magic fairy who will come along and pick up dirty dishes.

4   **I want to let someone else decide.**

Roman statesman and orator, Marcus Tullius Cicero, famously said that "More is lost by indecision than wrong decision." Of course, Cicero probably would have preferred an indecisive Mark

Anthony so he would not have been assassinated on December 7, 43 BC—but that is beside the point. Once captured by his enemies, Cicero allegedly said, "there is nothing proper about what you are doing, soldier, but do try to kill me properly." At that moment, Cicero preferred a decisive soldier so that his decapitation would be swift.

Like the third idea above, letting someone else make the decision is another pass the buck viewpoint. However, letting someone do your chores is not as serious as letting someone make your decisions. In fact, here you are deciding to NOT act. So, while some procrastinators will say they are simply indecisive, instead, they are willfully NOT making a decision. Like, on purpose. This can be particularly unnerving to those of us who are action-oriented organizers. My recommendation is to push decisions back to the procrastinators. You are not doing yourself or others a favor by doing everything yourself and making all the decisions. Like other organizations, families do not work well when led by dictatorships. If you allow family members to be indecisive, you end up raising and promoting passive-aggressive behavior that will become an impediment to future relationships and careers.

5   I fear that I will fail.

If you don't try, you cannot succeed. But for most procrastinators, the fear of failure is ever-looming. This is why some people don't want to clear out their stuff. What if something important gets thrown out? What if the new system I have created is terrible and I miss even more appointments? This fear becomes cyclical, so that the procrastinator continues to put off tasks and loses self-esteem and confidence in the process. Gently prodding your family members to take risks and try new organizational systems will help them become more confident and independent. Also, remind them that it is okay if something gets thrown out that needs to be replaced later. I use this mantra with my fearful ones:

"What is the worst thing that can happen here?" If the answers are not cancer or death, then we can fix the outcome if necessary.

6   This task is too hard.

Chronic procrastinators often make mountains out of molehills. For example, a task like calling your child's principal can become a huge task in your mind. "What if I say the wrong thing?" "How can I even get her to understand my viewpoint?" "What if I make things worse on the phone call?" Meanwhile, the school principal gets multiple parent phone calls and emails per day and is well versed in the process. Thus, there is no need for the parent to dramatize the situation; this same encounter happens all day long, all across American schools. The key here is to get the procrastinator to settle down and stop seeing everything as a monumental challenge. If you have children, I'm sure you have heard them catastrophize their boredom at some point in time. Savvy parents will not give into the drama and instead allow the kids to just be bored. It is not a big deal, and it is not a good reason to put off a task that will be perceived as a boring job. Similarly, if your family member says organizing is too hard, don't give into the drama. Instead, take his or her hand and tell them, "It's okay. We will start this together and soon you can do it on your own."

7   I don't see the vision.

Many people just don't see how organizing their sock drawers will transform their lives. These are the free spirits or dreamers of the family that just see no reason to give in to what they perceive to be an artificially induced order. This is where you need to investigate different aspects of your procrastinator's life. Is it taking too long for him or her to get ready in the morning? Could something be done in the living space that will make life easier or more pleasurable? You might even want to make a vision board or, at minimum, draw or define the overall vision. For my daughter, her vision was this scene: her, looking fantastic, walking to the college campus with her outfit on point, accessorized and having all the tools necessary to succeed in class, like headphones, a laptop, and her water bottle. Once the vision is clearly defined, your procrastinator might have more buy-in to the process of developing an organized life.

8   How do I even begin?

This is the easiest roadblock to remove. After all, you, the organized person, are present and accounted for. With input from your procrastinator, you can make a cheat sheet, a vision board and a road map that will lay out simple, clear instructions for him or her to begin the process of life organization.

Now that we understand why our families are bucking our attempts to help them stay organized and on task, we can begin to create real change. I had contemplated using the subtitle of "how to manipulate your family into adopting your organizational system." However, that is NOT what we are going to do. Much as I wish for my family to operate as a Wendy-dictatorship, they will not accord me that much power. Furthermore, the four of them can easily gang up on me. Instead, through the next several chapters I will discuss different techniques and systems that can work on your organizationally challenged family members. Because— remember—we all have the same goals: to live harmoniously in the same house and to live in a way that makes everyone happy.

While writing this book, I interviewed many of my friends and family members to get some more insight on how people perceived organization in their lives. Here are some interesting perspectives that might resonate with you in looking at your own households:

Viewpoint #1 (Amy):
I have worked very hard to become an organized person. I have had to discipline myself to stay organized because it can spiral very quickly. I have serious issues with things that need constant maintenance such

as dishes and laundry. My husband mostly does those repetitive things for me because I don't see finality to the task so it's hard for me to get motivated into doing it. I would let it pile up until it interfered with my daily life before I would do it. I have learned to downsize stuff and have a place for everything and keep all like items together—that is how I have organized my brain (and stuff) after LOTS of years of working on it. I also think that the way we grow up has a profound effect on how we approach housekeeping and organizing. I grew up in a house that had restricted rooms that people didn't go into because they might mess it up. A piece of fuzz on the carpet was unacceptable and my mom worried about people messing up vacuumed carpet lines. This made me miserable, and, I think, made me stop trying to keep the house perfect when my kids were growing up.

Viewpoint #2 (Kim):
I'm a master procrastinator. I do my best work at 2:00 am right before the deadline. I often wonder how much more effective I could be if I was one of those people who create a plan and then work the plan, but it's just not in my DNA. I've often wondered why I operate this way, but I think I might be addicted to the thrill of finishing just under a deadline. It's like running a race with myself. I do work that requires focus and I just think better at night. That's because, for me, there are fewer distractions, and for some reason, my brain is more creative and less transactional at night. During the day, each little thing takes immediate priority. Am I organized? Unintentionally so. I keep a mental list but seldom write it down. I like my surroundings organized but it doesn't bother me to be in clutter either. An organized space makes the transactional tasks easier to manage but I don't spend a lot of time organizing the big ideas— the creative things—until I'm doing the work. I find a natural peace in winding my way through a problem.

Viewpoint #3 (Lori):
I live with three other members on the ADHD spectrum. Here's what works for me: I do a countdown for my family to leave on time. We need to leave in 45 minutes, 30, 15 and 5. I always start at 45 minutes. I need to give every person in the family advance notice on things that

need to be completed. They need time to process everything. When the kids were little, I would lay out clothes and school supplies out in advance. I have friends that let their ADHD kids sleep in their school clothes which seemed to work with grade school aged kids. I don't help anyone search for items unless it is an emergency. I sit and wait for them. I'm not mad, I'm just waiting for them. I used to help but they would find the item and forget to tell me. Meanwhile, I'm still looking! So, instead, I'll patiently wait. In all situations, I must be direct with my ADHD family members. They don't always read people or situations well. In the end, I have had to let some things go. We might have a messy house, a late response to an event or just be rushing around at the last minute. It happens.

Viewpoint #4 (Alice):
When I have lots to do or want to do a lot of things at once, I just make lists on paper— the old-fashioned way really works! I do often lose the lists but then I simply make new ones! Just writing the list on paper clears out my head and makes it less stressful when I have lots to do. Also, when I have many errands, I write them all on a list, and in my head, I do this whole optimization thing where I map out the best strategy, so I don't do too many back-and-forth actions around town. Here's the thing—I'm not a big organizer girl, so I like to keep things simple, so I don't want to waste time organizing.

As you can see—we are all in this together, AND we all have different approaches to how we organize homes and life tasks. And know this now: you are NOT going to change your people. However, you can listen and learn and try to co-exist in a house that meets everyone's needs.

Before moving on to the next chapter, take some time to figure out if your family members are being defiant, procrastinating or exhibiting signs of ADHD. To deal with defiance, you might consider family therapy and finding ways to forge harmony in your household. For procrastination and ADHD, you will need to do some research and explore all different techniques to help everyone get focused and stay on task. We will explore these types of techniques in later chapters.

CHAPTER 3
CHEAT SHEET

Things to Know About Your ADHD People:
- They are creative and impulsive and are usually great at taking risks.
- They might exhibit symptoms of hyperactivity or daydreaming.
- Basic life tasks are often harder for them.
- They often have difficulty with executive functions, including remembering things, staying on task, managing time limits, and keeping focused.
- They might exhibit task-shifting, like changing from task to task without reaching completion on any of them.

Your ADHD people are important to you, so don't come down on them too hard or expect them to do things the same way as you. They might need counseling and medication to help them, but they also need a little more guidance from other family members. In later chapters, I will discuss how you can best assist them with your direct help or by finding them other assistance through body doubling, smartphone applications and other tips and tricks. For now, just recognize the differences and build up your patience so you can establish mutual respect and trust.

Reasons Why You Might Encounter Defiance from Your People:
- Your timing is bad.
- Your people do not know how to start the project.
- You have too high of expectations.
- Your people do not perceive the task as relevant or important.
- Your people do not understand your system.

- You probably have seen the t-shirt that says, "It's not me. It's you." However, defiance in the family is not that black and white of a situation. Sometimes it is them who are in the wrong, but sometimes it is YOU! Or as I like to say in these situations to my family members: "You were right. I was less right." Again, the key here is to establish open communication. If your family members are truly in the wrong and wreaking havoc in the home, consult a licensed professional for assistance.

Procrastinator Viewpoints to Counteract:
- I can do it tomorrow.
- I work better under pressure.
- I know someone else will do the task for me.
- I want to let someone else make decisions for me.
- I fear that I will fail this task.
- I think this task is too hard for me.
- I don't see the overall vision.
- I don't know what step to take first.

Ahhhh—procrastinators. They love to hype up the issue and make it part of their identity. This is not a book about procrastination, but I do address some techniques in later chapters that will assist you with family members who keep trying to put off life tasks. Procrastination is a long running, created habit that is often hard for family members to change. Since it becomes a defining personality trait for them, you are not going to be successful by taking a negative or adversarial stand on procrastination. Instead, seek out more knowledge on the subject or consider cognitive behavior feedback to help those individuals learn new, more productive habits. In the meantime, you can work on your own patience and investigate some different techniques that might provide a forward path for everyone.

(4)

HOW TO GET STARTED

As the organizer of your family home, you have probably already attempted several ways to instill order. Over the years, I tried all the tips and tricks, including color-coded bins, new closet systems, whiteboards, notes all over the house and simply throwing things out when the other family members were out of the house. However, the problem with all these systems was ME. They were established by me, decreed by me, and implemented by me. My family could care less about these systems.

Instead, take the time now to work through several factors to set your family up for success.

- **Analyze your family members and their attitudes towards organization and schedules.** Observe your family and figure out their organizational personalities and love languages. If family members have ADHD, read up on the disorder and help them get treatment. If your family members are severe hoarders, obtain professional assistance from mental health providers. See where you differ and where you agree on home organization. Really look at your family members and try to see where they are coming from and how they learn and look at the world.

For example, if you are dealing with sentimental souls, see what drives their need to collect. If you have family members with ADHD, observe them trying to get ready for work or school and take note of how easily distracted they are with issues that pop up along the way. Your observations and insights now will help you figure out ways to help them when it comes time to act on house organization and personal scheduling.

- **Give everyone some grace.** If you have been yelling, demanding, or annoying everyone with your organizational mantras and systems, ask for forgiveness and try to forge some common ground. Tell everyone that you are in the frame of mind to listen so that you can all develop a way to deal with family chaos and be happier.

  Obviously, this is going to be an ongoing struggle for you—the organized one of the family. You are going to need to be on your A game and try to catch yourself before you yell, nag, or react badly to your family's struggles with organization. When situations arise where you just can't believe that your son's room exploded in dirty dishes overnight or that your significant other brought home another box of glassware from the thrift store, take a moment to just breathe. Is it worth a big blow out fight or is this something that you can gently mention at another time when your son can't find a clean dish in the kitchen or when your spouse is frustrated by the too-full kitchen cabinet? The goal is less chaos and more overall happiness for everyone. Don't get caught up in little details.

- **Take a tour of your home.** Now is the time to walk around and map out all the areas of the home, inside and out. You will have your specific hot button areas, like the kitchen and the laundry room, but there are all sorts of areas that might be more important to your other family members. Ask your family members to walk with you and have everyone try to see the home with fresh eyes. You might even ask a trusted friend or extended family member to come over and talk to your family about what he or she notices when walking around your house.

Just recently, my adult daughter and her husband came home for the holidays and provided some insight into our living room area rug. Let me give you some backstory—my husband and I had a long running issue with our very nice living room rug. Our elderly dog was starting to have too many accidents and these episodes were ruining our rug. We did all sorts of things to try to save the expensive thing—baking soda, pet urine destroyer products, steam cleaning, and more. We took the rug outside and brushed it out and let it air out for days. But of course, the scent lingered. I hated to even sit in the living room and definitely could no longer do my stretching workout on that rug. My husband, however, thought that the rug was fine, and we could just keep cleaning it periodically. When my daughter came home for the holidays, she immediately noticed the odor. When my husband expressed surprise, Anna-Claire responded very logically that we probably did not notice because we were used to the smell. Later that day, my husband said, "let's go online and order one of those washable rugs to get us through with Mr. Pringles." Once he had some outside confirmation of the issue, my husband was ready to take action and get rid of that rug, even though it was a beautiful furnishing that looked great in our living room.

Having outside confirmation of your problem areas is very helpful. However, get outside opinions, also, on what areas work well in the home. You might be surprised by what people will tell you. My neighbor recently invited several of us over to help her arrange her living room furniture. She was stuck on how to best arrange the room. We all threw out ideas and she latched onto the ones she liked and discarded the rest. We gave her a lot of praise for her entry way table and lamp which surprised her since she was uncertain of how it looked next to her new wallpaper. Having that confirmation gave her some confidence and meant that she could leave that space alone and spend more time on the other areas in the home.

Once you get some internal and external opinions, make sure you write down all the different viewpoints. In addition, it is helpful to sketch out a floor plan or list each room; this preliminary work will help you all with the next task.

- **Hold a family meeting and discuss everyone's goals.** This piggybacks off the last step where you went around making observations. Now it is time to apply the observations and make some concrete plans. Of course, you know your own goals, but do you know about your family members' concerns? Are there areas of the home or life that your people are struggling to manage? By talking to your family, you will uncover new areas that require organizational help. For example, my in-laws recently moved houses and one challenge for them was compiling and managing all their important documents. And on a recent trip to a local craft store, my husband expressed the desire to come up with systems for managing his photographs and sentimental memorabilia. He wanted to start buying bins and containers, but we had to rein in that impulse. Right now, you are just gathering information.

When I did this planning with my family, I found out that my husband was stressed out by our kitchen cabinets. Where I had everything stuffed away inside and knew where everything was located, he was at a loss. He didn't know where things were and when he started opening cabinets, everything started falling out. This was the impetus we needed to overhaul our kitchen organization, pulling things out and eliminating items that were rarely or never used. I took Todd's advice and moved the bowls to an area close to the stove, so they were in easy reach of soup pots. This seems like such a little thing, but it removed a constant irritant from his life. In the past, the bowls were in a drawer near the pantry for cereal access, but our kids were mostly grown, and cereal was not such a big part of our lives. It is amazing how the little changes can impact our lives by simply removing obstacles and making things easier as we go throughout the day.

- **Use these goals to create a mission statement or vision board.** You don't have to write out a formal statement or design a vision board, but these items might provide focus and motivation for everyone. A vision board is particularly appealing to family members who are visual creatures. For example, if your son wants a clean, dedicated space for doing artwork, you might find pictures in magazines or on the internet that show spaces where crayons, colored pencils, paper, and craft supplies are all sorted and looking fabulous. For your athletic daughter, you might sketch out a wall in your garage where all her sport supplies are shown hanging up neatly on hooks, ready for her next adventure.

  Creating a positive visual or mission statement sets the tone for your whole operation. If you have been having fights about stuff or territory wars in your home, the pretty vision board can be a peace offering where all sides come to just one overall agreement. The other stuff, like how to get this beautiful vision, will come later. For now, you just need everyone to agree to one nice, non-chaotic home vision.

- **Listen and establish trust.** One member of our extended family has a lot of stuff. I mean, A LOT OF STUFF. He is not really hoarding but has collected many things over the years and is generally paralyzed with the task of needing to downsize items so that properties can be cleaned and sold. This is an area fraught with emotional issues. The children want things organized or removed but they don't want to fight with their father. In turn, the father has a lot of emotions wrapped up in the items. There are stories to tell about the objects. Also, he has concerns about getting rid of items that cost a lot of money over the years. There were family debates held and talk of dumpsters, yard sales and auctions. But really, those things were all endings, not beginnings. To start, the children had to establish trust. This meant going with their father to the properties and looking at all the items and listening to stories. NOTHING was moved or thrown away. That is not where you begin. I have read a lot of organizational books that start with the suggestion that you enter the area with black trash bags and donation boxes. However, if you are dealing with several different personalities and ways of organizing spaces, you cannot begin with trash duty. That is the surefire way of alienating people and causing arguments.

If you only retain one thing from this book on how to get your family to agree to better house and life organization, remember that TRUST is the lynchpin to everything. If you have been arguing about stuff, throwing away things willy-nilly, moving stuff without permission, or talking smack about each other's way of living, then trust has been eroded. Take time to listen to each other and get trust back in place.

- **Make a good list.** Ask each family member to write down main areas of organizational concern. Or, alternatively, present everyone with a list and ask them to circle everything that they would like to see organized.

It is easy to impose your ideas on your family. I simply wanted all the dirty clothes put in the laundry room, all the bedroom closets to be manageable and all the living room areas kept nice. When I interviewed my family members, however, I found out what challenged them daily. For example, one child was upset that she did not have all the index cards, staplers, and notebooks in one area for her schoolwork. Another child wanted a better system for her make-up area, so she would have room to do her daily routine. The last child simply wanted to be able to always find her shoes. My husband wanted nice, curated collection display areas and the ability to find what he always wanted in the kitchen junk drawer. He also wanted us to pare down our plastic food container drawer and make it easy for him to always find a plate or soup bowl. This was fascinating to me. As a chronic organizer and picker upper, I just had a vision of clean lines and no clutter in my home. But my family members had real concerns and annoyances that impacted them daily. This meeting also helped me see that while I prided myself on keeping the home looking good, I was also contributing to the problem by throwing things away that were needed or stuffing everything into cabinets and drawers where the mess kept people from finding things and being productive.

Here is a list of common home and organizational areas that might be annoying your family members. You could ask them to rate each item so that you, as a family, know where to begin:

- Coat closet
- Junk drawer
- Kitchen utensil drawer
- Pantry
- School supply area
- File cabinets
- Garage
- Car(s)
- Camper
- Boat
- Storage container
- Shed
- Basement
- Attic
- Bedroom(s)
- Clothes closet
- Laundry room
- Jewelry box
- Important documents
- Photographs
- Sentimental collections
- Family historical objects and documents
- Children's artwork
- Hobby rooms and craft areas
- Sports equipment areas
- Make-up/Cosmetic areas
- Bathroom drawers
- Gift wrap areas
- Playrooms and toyboxes
- Under sink cabinets
- Cleaning supply areas
- Pots, pans, and dishes areas
- Outdoor shed or garden areas
- Family calendars and schedules
- Front/back yards
- Patio/Outdoor area
- Desks
- Home office
- Bedside tables
- TV cabinet/Media area
- Living room

In addition to organizational items, you might consider and write down cleaning tasks as well. If you are cleaning out the basement, you might add on the task of sweeping the floors or wiping off shelving. If the backyard is an area of concern to someone, you might add on the need to weed or mulch landscaping. Now is the time to get everyone's wish list. The more dreaming and planning you do up front will pay off in the long term. I know some organizational gurus simply recommend that you declutter and sort and don't worry about cleaning tasks. However, the goal is an orderly home without chaos. By taking the time to do the task thoroughly right now, you and the rest of the family will see a completed vision. Leaving a task just part way done runs a high risk of never achieving completion. Also, adding in the cleaning tasks to your goals right now ensures that when you schedule the time to tackle the area, you will break the job down into manageable chunks of time and ultimately have enough time to do everything. So, while the first list tackles organizational needs, the second list will be the ancillary services needed to complete the vision.

Some of these tasks include:

- Removing all trash
- Wiping down shelves
- Sweeping floors
- Wiping out drawers
- Weeding exterior areas
- Mulching landscaping
- Trimming bushes and trees
- Vacuuming vehicles
- Wiping down interiors of vehicles
- Washing down woodwork
- Washing windows

Research has shown that writing down your goals ensures a greater chance of success. Neuropsychologists call this practice the "generation effect" since self-generated material results in better recall than merely reading or listening to information. Thus, not only will a written list provide a visual cue for things that need done, but the list will also help you remember and complete tasks. This is because the act of writing generates information that gets encoded in our brains better than just ideas we think about or discuss. Multiple research studies have proven that people who take notes at meetings, classes and interviews recall important information more often than other people who just listen and try to remember. The cognitive process of listening, thinking, and writing down facts makes more important connections in the brain.

This generation effect is why all the spiritual gurus advocate that followers write down their goals or make vision boards to manifest positive future events. In fact, when I made my 2023 New Year's Eve resolutions, I kept a manifesting journal where I wrote down the good things that I wanted to happen in the new year. At first, I felt ridiculous writing the journal and trying to manifest future events. However, one of my positive visions was to write a book which I had been trying to do unsuccessfully for the past ten years. I had a defeatist attitude about said book. However, after writing things down and posting inspiring notes to my computer, I was prompted to pull up my old file and, by golly, two months later I had a finished book that I then published entitled, *Lessons from the Landlady: How to Avoid My Mistakes and Be Successful in Real Estate*. So now—I'm a believer! On January 1, get out that journal or bust out your craft supplies and make an epic vision board. In the meantime, write down everything your family members identify as areas that need to be organized and items that need to be cleaned. Research shows that this written list has the propensity to help you achieve your goals better than simply just discussing the tasks.

Every morning when my husband and I walk the dog, Todd likes to talk about his hopes and dreams for the future and basically all the other creative ideas that he has floating around in his head. As a goal-oriented person, I started to get antsy after several months of all talk and no action. I think I even blurted out, "Can we have less talking and more doing?" I was tired of hearing how he wanted to reorganize his art supplies or set up a work room in the basement. I had already offered up my help for what felt like a thousand times. You might be in a similar situation with the dreamers in your family. They are wildly creative and have the best ideas; however, their follow-through is nonexistent. Again, your people are being held back by their ADHD, their lack of focus, their fear of failure, their inability to find the first step, their perfectionism, or their laziness. When I learned to reign in my impatience with Todd and instead suggest that he write down his ideas so that he could remember them and refine them—we started to see progress. Once Todd wrote down the ideas, he started to see them as projects instead of just wishes for the future. The next week he had enlisted people to move things and to help him get him organized. And in a few months, he had a dedicated workspace where he created amazing resin art pieces for everyone for the holidays using real silver trays and watch cases and filling them with dried flowers and vintage jewelry. Todd's dreams were fun for him to muse on and talk about, but they didn't become reality until he wrote down his ideas, made lists of things he needed to do and took small, active steps towards his goal.

- **Determine if anything can be outsourced.** So, here's the thing about being an organizational freak— you might be tempted to tackle everything yourself. We have already discussed the need to tread lightly so you can get buy-in from the other family members. In addition to listening to everyone's concerns, you must decide NOT to be the scheduling and organizing martyr. First, it's too much work and a hassle for you to take on alone. I'm sure, like me, you have more important things to do than organize the entire house and create everyone's life schedules. Secondly, this martyrdom just won't work in the long run. Your systems will only be understood and kept up by **you** and everything will soon fall back into chaos.

Some of the items on your family's to-do list are probably things that can be outsourced. If you have the means, consider hiring someone to assist in a big spring cleaning or in carrying items to take to a charitable organization. In my town, we have a charity shop that will come to your home and haul away your donations for free. In the urban area where my mother lives, there is an active neighborhood Facebook page where people can post pictures of items they want to give away. People then simply put the stuff on their porches and neighbors come and pick up the items. No gas money needed and no pulled muscles in hauling that couch to the Salvation Army.

If paperwork is a concern, you can hire people to file for you or compile all your items in binders. Old photographs and slides can be given to companies like ScanDigital or ScanCafe, that will digitize everything so you can more easily share the memorabilia and save space. If you have items to sell, you can find people who will advertise your items on Facebook marketplace or eBay. If you have a lot of items or some big-ticket items, you can call an auctioneer who will sell your items at auction for a percentage. Sure, you could try to sell it yourself, but an expert with a captive audience is going to get a bigger price overall and you will not have the hassle of advertising and finding a buyer. When my children were in high school and college, they took on the task of holding Saturday morning yard sales to make money for shopping sprees and vacations. It was a great win-win for the entire extended family; we all got rid of items we didn't want while the kids provided the muscle power and made all the profit. I particularly liked not having to drive everything to the charities who would accept the items since the kids managed the sale and got rid of everything at the end. I will address more information about selling and donating items in Chapter 10.

Some tasks can even be outsourced within the family to each other. If you particularly enjoy a certain task then simply state that you want to be the person who performs it, like doing all the laundry for the family. Someone else might love gardening and choose to care for all the outdoor work. In my family, my middle daughter has excellent penmanship and she liked writing things on our family whiteboard in different colored markers. There is no need to make everyone do everything. We all have different talents and interests. Allow your family members to step up and take on some of these tasks. The home only works if everyone participates and works toward the common goal. Again— that goal is non-chaos and happiness for all.

CHAPTER 4 CHEAT SHEET

Here's a recap of the eight preliminary steps to tackling the chaos in your home:

1. **Analyze your family's organizational personalities.**

   Do your research on ADHD, procrastination, collecting and hoarding. Look into professional medical help where needed. Try to see things from other perspectives.

2. **Give everyone some grace.**

   Take a deep breath when faced with organizational and scheduling challenges with your family members. Try to keep from yelling, nagging, or complaining and instead listen to their concerns.

3. **Sketch a floor plan of your home, inside and outside.**

   Try to get everyone in the house to look at your dwelling areas with new eyes, seeing the areas that need the most organizing help. Ask extended family and friends for their insights on your home organization.

4. **Hold a family meeting to discuss organizational goals.**

   Ask everyone to vocalize their individual goals for the home. Listen to everyone and write down all ideas.

5. **Create a mission statement or vision board.**

   Create a visually appealing map, list or graphic that represents the goals the family discussed at your meeting. Hang this in a prominent place or make color copies for everyone.

6   **Listen and establish trust.**

Don't plow ahead without making sure that everyone feels secure in the plan and trusts the process. Check in with everyone periodically to make sure that you are all on the same page.

7   **Make a good list of everyone's organizational needs and wants.**

If you don't write things down, your home organization project will never happen. Gently remind your group that talking time is over and plans need to be written down and executed.

8   **Determine if anything can be outsourced.**

Let your family members volunteer for the tasks that they enjoy or perform particularly well. If you have the financial means, consider paying some outside support for more difficult or more time-consuming tasks, or just as a way to get the organization process started.

(5)

DON'T GET RID OF ANYTHING

Now that you have talked to your family and researched all the options available to you for obtaining help and resources in your community, it is time to begin. As an organized person, you might be tempted to start grabbing cluttery items and throwing them into donation boxes and trash bags. **But be patient.** It is still not time for that yet. Believe me, I'm on your side. I love throwing out stuff that is no longer needed or wanted. But remember, these items are in the family home. Someone else might need or want them.

And one little family meeting isn't going to cut it. I wish that talking one time about our goals and aspirations would turn the whole chaotic family around, but that simply is not the case. And you know this deep down in your heart too.

So here we go—back to those eight steps above. But now we go into more depth on a couple of the tasks.

- **Refine your assessment.** I asked you to consider your family members and their organizational personalities. Off the top of your head, you know which one is a sentimental soul, which one is a procrastinator, and which one loves to color code the clothing in her closet. However, there are more in-depth viewpoints that will affect how each person decides to organize items and tackle life issues. And your cursory analysis of each person will not reflect his or her comprehensive vision of home life.

Here are some questions to ask yourself and your family members.
You can do this formally or informally, but getting these answers will help you gauge the buy-in for the family vision and help you gently prod each member to pull his or her weight in your organizational journey.

Questions to assess how everyone feels about routines and schedules:
- How do you tackle daily tasks?
- Do you keep a calendar?
- Do you keep a daily to-do list?
- Do you like checking off tasks?

Questions to assess how everyone feels about personal possessions:
- Do you like seeing all your items at once or do you like to put things away?
- Do you like displaying objects or having a clear space devoid of items?
- Do you have collections or sentimental things that need preserved?
- Do you have trouble letting go of things?
- Do you like to sell items for money?
- Do you like giving items away to friends or charitable organizations?

Questions to assess everyone's threshold for clutter:
- Are there areas of the house that feel cluttered or over-furnished?
- Are there areas of the house that feel too stark or impersonal?
- How do you feel when you go into your bedroom?
- What is the best room in the house? Why?
- What is the worst room in the house? Why?
- Where do you feel most comfortable in the house?
- Where do you feel least comfortable in the house?

Finding out the answers to these questions will help you in refining your plan to manage the chaos. Once you know what you are dealing with in terms of doing a big organizational shift in your household, it is time to go to the next step.

- **Establish trust again.** Throughout the process it is important to keep checking in with your people. Since you are an organization guru, the past may not have always endeared you to the rest of the family. Perhaps, like me, you once threw out someone's favorite hoodie or got rid of all the papers that looked like trash on the mantle, only to find out that buried within was a very important paper with the key to someone's personal success. These were not your finest moves, in their opinion, but these tasks were in the interest of clutter-free living for you! Thus, you need to revisit the trust issue AGAIN.

    One great way to establish trust is to set up some family guidelines. For example, you might institute the rule that you will not throw away anything without approval (this one was particularly hard for me!) Another good one is to try not to pass judgment during the organizational process, such as wondering aloud why your husband needs all that workout equipment when he never works out. Believe me, these things need to be addressed, but we can find a kinder way to get to these issues in later chapters.

- **Identify the important tasks.** Now that you have everyone's personalities and opinions accounted for and trust is in place, it is time to separate tasks into two categories: important and less important. By looking at everyone's opinions, you can more easily identify the tasks that take precedence. If all members of your family have identified the kitchen as your messiest room with the most amount of stress, then that will become the most important task.

- **Write it all down.** This is a great job for the most organized and motivated member of your family. However, if you have someone with great penmanship and artistic aesthetic, you might want that person to write down the goals in a gorgeous way or to draw a roadmap or vision board that beautifully depicts the entire project.

It is important that everyone has access to these two lists. Therefore, you might consider writing them on a chalkboard painted wall, a big whiteboard, or a bulletin board. Or you might draw it out and make color copies, so everyone has their own lists. You never know, someone might be so motivated that he or she will start to tackle some of the list items spontaneously. Probably not, but there is always hope!

I know you are getting antsy and really want to start buying organization bins, labels, and different colored Sharpie markers, but HOLD OFF! The more groundwork you do in preparing the family, the more headway you will make in controlling your household chaos. Plus, there is no need to buy anything until you go through stuff you already have! Believe me, I have gone down the road of buying all the beautiful stuff to hold all our junk. Unfortunately, a lot of these beautiful containers went right into our next yard sale. You do not know yet what you will be dealing with until after you complete your two lists of tasks, so don't waste your time and money.

CHAPTER 5 CHEAT SHEET

Thus, to recap here, you want to do these tasks before we start the real work of decluttering, rearranging, and organizing:

- Listen to your family members and try to understand their world views.

- Establish trust with your family members AGAIN.

- Make two lists: Important and Less Important.

- Do a beautiful visual representation of these two lists that everyone can access.

(6)

IF YOU DON'T SCHEDULE IT, IT WILL NEVER HAPPEN

FINALLY! We can begin. Well, not quite yet. Put down the black trash bags and hold off on collecting boxes from work. First, we must schedule when the organization work begins. Notice that I said "schedule." You will not have everyone drop everything at one of your planning sessions and start hauling out broken furniture. As they say, Rome was not built in a day and your chaotic life will not be fixed overnight. Since these tasks involve touching everyone else's stuff, it is only fair that those affected have a voice as to when the touching and rearranging starts.

Doing the schedule means you need to go back to your personal assessments of your family members. Since you have listened intently to everyone and heard how each one approaches clutter and organization, you can now consider how to best proceed. Should you pick a rainy day to start? Is there a time of year when no one is playing sports, and everyone seems to be home more often? Would the family rather do small spurts of 30 minutes here and there or are they likely to get into the task and want to block off an afternoon? Would it be more motivating to choose some seasonal dates? For example, as my children were growing up, I instituted a wardrobe clean out each summer before back-to-school shopping day and a toy room and bedroom clean out right before Christmas when I knew that Santa (that stuff enabler!) would be dropping off more stuff to the household.

The main thing now is to pull out the calendars and get definitive times and dates scheduled for everyone. Put on more times and dates than you think you will need. Don't worry— you will not run out of work and that way some dates can be canceled as other things come up. After all, you are not going to clean out the garage when you could be attending a neighbor's barbecue instead. You will need some flexibility. I like to clean up stuff, but I like having fun more, and so does your family.

There are a thousand ways to do this schedule. If your family members are mostly teens or adults, you can do a few tasks together and then let them go forth on their own when possible. Young children, of course, will need full management from you. However, I have also found that my ADHD child and my lover-of-stuff husband both require some handholding as well. Thus, our organization sessions must be scheduled with multiple people there on hand. I have even enlisted other people to come and help if the task was monumental, like packing up items for college or sorting through and cataloguing all my husband's Atari cartridges. Some people, like my in-laws who require help with paperwork, will simply prefer to outsource that task to someone else willing to do it for free or payment. Therefore, some items on the calendar may just be hiring others to do organizational work.

Once you have some calendar dates, it is time to assign tasks from your two lists so that everyone knows what you are tackling that day. While it seems intuitive to begin with the most important task, you might want to choose, instead, a task that is more easily completed.

This accomplishes a couple of things. First, you gain a win for the family. This will build confidence and show that the tasks ahead of you all are achievable. Second, you will provide motivation. If the kitchen junk drawer was the first job and everyone raves over how easily they can find batteries, paperclips, and bandages, then they might be better motivated to complete a couple more areas.

As the main organizer of the family, you may be tempted to simply do everything yourself. After all, you are motivated and willing to do the work. But, trust me, you are not doing anyone any favors here. When you send your kids off to college or the work world, do you want them ready to adjust to a strange new world with a skill set of organization and scheduling that they learned from home? Or do you plan to continue to put alerts on their cell phones and drive to campus every week to do their laundry, clean their dorm rooms and help them make study schedules? And if your significant other is not fully involved, you run the risk of resenting him or her. In turn, your spouse will think you are not respecting him or her when you start moving everything around and throwing things away.

CHAPTER 6 CHEAT SHEET

To create a great schedule, consider these items:
- Discuss the best times and dates with your family.
- Write down these times and dates on everyone's calendars.
- Assign tasks to the dates from your two lists.
- Do NOT do everything yourself.

(7)

TIME TO DEPLOY THE TROOPS AND UTILIZE DIFFERENT ORGANIZATIONAL STRATEGIES TO CONTROL CLUTTER

Now that you are scheduled, it is time to discuss some cool ways to get your crew to organize stuff and stay one step ahead of chaos. Most people think of organization as putting all like-minded things together and buying cool contraptions and containers to look beautiful. I thought the same thing—hence why I wanted to decant juices in my refrigerator into pretty glass pitchers even though my family rarely drinks fruit juices. I think we all fall prey to the cute little organizational items in Target and the gimmicky drawer organizers, like sock sorting grids and felt jewelry drawer containers. Not to disparage those items, because they can be a nice reward at the end of the process (which we will discuss in another chapter), but the goal is to get everyone in the family on the same page and to give everyone some tools to better succeed in life.

In fact, I think the most important work has already occurred. Your family has talked about the importance of a clean, orderly home. You have listened to each other and discovered the stressors that each family member wants to overcome. You have made a master plan and scheduled times to work on organizational projects. **Look at what all you have accomplished!**

Now it is time to talk about the strategies that can help your ADHD and collector family members get organized and STAY ORGANIZED.

As people say, there is more than one way to skin a cat. I honestly have no idea why we say that phrase, but you know what I mean. But I can't help it—after I typed those lines, I had to look up the origins of that weird saying. Mark Twain evidently popularized the "skin a cat" phrasing, but the original wording had even earlier and creepier roots. In the 1600s, people often said there were more ways to kill a dog than hanging and more ways to kill a cat than choking it with cream. I'm not sure why we equate having multiple options with various ways to kill pets, but I'm not in charge of common sayings, so please do not put angry reviews on Amazon saying that I hate pets. That is not true; I have a lovely dog, Mr. Pringles, who would beg to differ. But back to organizing—there are several ways to achieve your goals; the challenge is finding the path that your family can best follow. Changing your whole world outlook, as we have already discussed, will not be easy, and to do so, this organization thing might take many circuitous routes.

So, here— in no particular order— are some strategies to employ when facing the clutter zones in your home:

Do You Still Love It? (The "Spark Joy" Approach)

As you are students of organizational systems, I'm sure you have come across the bestselling book, *the life-changing magic of tidying up* by Marie Kondo. In the book, Kondo elaborates on the Japanese art of decluttering and organizing. If you have ever seen Kondo's television show or read the book, you know that her famous question to ask clients when decluttering objects is, "Does this spark joy?" Basically, you hold each item you own in your hand and ask yourself if it inspires joy in your life. If so, the item stays. If not, the item is discarded with heartfelt thanks. Kondo actually prompts her clients to say, "thank you" to the item being removed, like "thank you scarf for keeping my neck warm in the winter."

I have found that a modified version of the joy approach works great with my wardrobe cleansing. Clothes that do not make me feel good about myself, just fit weirdly, are too hard to clean or too difficult to button up in back by myself are NOT joyful and should leave my closet. After all, I wear the same things that I love over and over, and I enjoy buying a few new items each season.

Recently I went through my bookshelves and employed the same process. I had been holding onto book titles from college, even books that I didn't really enjoy reading the first time. Thus, I knew that I would not be re-reading those books. And, since I'm now in my 50s and on a different career path, I will not need these books with my notations to teach any English classes. If I do teach English again, I'm only going to choose titles that "spark joy," because life is too short to read *Moby Dick*. I can sum it up for you: The captain gets obsessed with killing a whale that bit off his leg. There are lots of chapters about that obsession. In the end, the captain harpoons the whale, who then majestically takes down the boat, killing the entire crew, except Ishmael, the narrator (convenient, so there is someone left to tell the story). I don't need all that revenge angst in my life. (If you did your honors thesis on the novel *Moby Dick* or re-read it every year for fun, please do not send me hate mail. I'm glad it sparks joy for you!) As a previous English major and lover of reading, going through my books seemed like a ridiculous proposition. After all, I'm the same person who used to tell everyone that I didn't trust people who have zero books in their homes. I'm also the same person who is now less judgmental and who reads all her books on an iPad. I'm also empty nesting, downsizing my stuff and simplifying life. Therefore, the non-joyful books needed to go. I packed up 15 boxes of books and dropped them off at the Goodwill which felt both rewarding and liberating.

Sparking joy is a lovely way to say that your clothing should be comfortable, should keep you cool in summer and warm in winter and should make you feel like a million bucks. Your home décor should be soothing, inspiring, and engaging. Your kitchen dishes, glassware and mugs should be useful and pretty because you use them every day. Your stuff should make you happy! If it doesn't, then you need to remove the items from your home. In later chapters, I will discuss object burden where you hold on to items that make you feel guilty or bad. These items do the opposite of sparking joy; they actively cause you distress and need to go.

My sister-in-law recently emptied out her attic and had a yard sale. As she purveyed the proliferation of toddler furniture and toys (her kids are in high school!), she turned to her husband and asked, "Why did we keep all of this stuff?" I'm guessing it is because at one point in time, all that stuff sparked joy—joy in the laughter of her kids playing with the toys and joy at being a parent and tucking said children into their beds at night. Now the kids were in high school, creating havoc as teenagers do, and sparking joy in different ways—in school successes and volleyball wins. It was time to let go of the past and it was liberating to reclaim all that attic space. And tripping over all the piles of stuff was NOT sparking joy at home. In fact, it was becoming a fire hazard as other stuff needed to be stored in the attic and the original piles were taking up valuable real estate. This example brings me to my next approach to organization. . .

The Valuable Real Estate Approach

Some people find that talking about the process of sparking joy and thanking objects is just a little too corny (my husband) and they would rather look at the problem in a more logical manner. Also, the sparking joy approach doesn't work in all instances. For example, my kitchen is not my happy place. I cook to eat healthy and not go out to eat all the time, but cooking, in general, is not joyful to me. I do like it on the holidays when all my kids are home and we are hanging out, drinking wine and baking, but on a daily basis—no, I don't think so. Since I would rather be reading, writing, walking or basically anything instead of cooking dinner, I see cooking implements and ingredients as a type of drudgery.

Therefore, I approach my kitchen with a more pragmatic approach. There is one drawer near the stove to hold all my cooking implements like spatulas, wooden spoons, measuring cups and such. That drawer is "valuable real estate." Some items just have no business being in there. I literally use a meat thermometer once per year when making the Thanksgiving turkey, so I don't need to stumble upon it daily when I'm going after my stainless-steel spatula that flips my eggs perfectly. Also, I don't need 18 soup ladles since at most, I'm serving from three pots total and that's just when I'm hosting an event.

Cleaning out a single drawer or cabinet, then, is the perfect opportunity to put into practice the valuable real estate approach. Since you have your container: the drawer, cabinet, or cupboard, already established, you know that you can only fit in so many items. And once you meet the threshold, which for me, is a little "under" filled so you can see items and move them around easily, then you are DONE.

This valuable real estate system seems so easy but will bring grown men (like my husband) to their knees. "What do you mean there's no more room?" "Why can't I keep all six of these hammers?" "I might need this cable cord and I won't know where it is if I can't keep it in this drawer." These are all real laments that I have heard when employing this approach. This is when you must get crafty with your next steps in the process.

So, in the case of my important kitchen drawer that is right by the stove, one valid technique is to leave everything out on the counter and let a week or two go by. Only the items that get used on a regular basis get to live in that valuable real estate. The remainder of the items are "occasional" use and must move to another space, a space that is not "stove-front." And the items that are never used, like the third string spatulas, can get donated or trashed.

This is a system that can literally get employed in any area of your home. For clothing, I keep track of items that don't get worn each year. I assess my clothing at the beginning of each season change and adjust shoes and clothing accordingly. I know some people who do the hanger trick where they place all hangers backwards in the closet and when items are taken out and worn, they flip the hangers around correctly. This way you know definitively at the end of the season what items were not worn and can be removed from the closet. For my closet, I just use observation. If some clothing items are costume or formal wear that I might need on occasion, they can move to another area of the home since they are not main wardrobe worthy. However, regular clothing that doesn't get worn all spring needs to be sold or donated because there is a reason that I didn't wear it this spring; clearly, the clothing item is uncomfortable, not flattering, dated or ill-fitting. On very rare occasions, the item is not worn because there is nothing to coordinate with those crazy yellow corduroy pants. On those occasions, I need to decide to either cut my losses and sell/donate—or take the time, money and effort to find matching items for those pants. This is a moment to go back to that "does it inspire joy" procedure. If the pants are fantastic, pull them out and go shopping to find coordinating items. If they are pretty but not worth more money and effort, then donate or sell those pants.

There is valuable real estate all over your home. Your go-to drawer in the laundry room, the medicine cabinet, the bedside stand, your pantry, the coffee table in your living room, the hall closet, your garden shed, etc. You might want to make a list of all your hot spots so that you can best plan the items that should fill those spaces. Next, empty out each hot spot and clean the cabinet, drawer, shed, or table. Now, look at that prime real estate. What can you do to improve that area? Maybe a drawer could use some dividers or organizers to let you see the stuff better. Maybe a shed or alcove could get some better shelving or lighting. Maybe some things need a fresh coat of paint or some pretty drawer liner/paper to keep the space looking clean and spiffy. Do those things now. Thus, you have just renovated your prime real estate and you do not want to fill that prime place with trash. Take the time now to ONLY put in the items that you use regularly and need to find in that location. After all, million-dollar properties at the beach do not hold onto junky and broken items, so use this time to evict those items from your luxury real estate places in your home.

Currently, I have a block on tackling my cosmetics area in my bathroom. I am blessed to have a lovely sit-down area to do makeup and hair. However, right now, I have a variety of different skin regime products and cosmetics scattered around the counter, along with hot rollers, nail polishes, brushes, combs and a big antique mirror that has sat on my cosmetics table for the past 15 years. Over the holidays, my oldest daughter, Maddie, pointed out that the mirror is not very effective because of how it has silvered with age. She also highlighted the fact that the mirror is big and takes up a lot of valuable space. "Mom," she said, "you could get rid of that thing and put in a modern mirror that you can see in and that takes up less space." I know she is right. This space is used every day and is, for sure, valuable real estate. That old mirror has hung out there for a long time because it is pretty cool, but it is not adding any practical value. In fact, the mirror is detracting from the space because I can't see myself in it! I need to find a new home for the mirror and allow my space to better meet my daily needs.

There might be items that you want to hold onto for a rainy day or for a future project. These items do not live in your valuable spots. Similarly, seasonal stuff can live in basements and attics but only if they spark joy and still get used. It is okay to keep formal attire in your closet if you have room for the items. After all, you should not get rid of the great cocktail dress that you will wear to some formal event in the future. However, if you rarely go out to such occasions, it is okay to eliminate it from your life right now. In the future, you can borrow or buy a dress if some occasion does arise. My stepfather, John, gleefully got rid of all his suits and ties when he retired from work. When my daughters recently got married, John simply went to the thrift store and bought a tweed jacket and tie to wear for the day. Afterwards, he simply re-donated the attire. Problem solved. There is no need to keep things around "just because" or for rare future events. In my neighborhood, we regularly borrow stockpots, crockpots, chafing dishes, water pitchers, wine glasses, coolers and more from each other. Why keep a ton of stuff around when you only throw a graduation party once or twice? I only need two big pots for soup. If I'm having an occasion where I decide to make three soups, I simply hit up a family member or friend for that third pot. No need to clutter up valuable real estate with occasional items.

Using the prime real estate approach with your organizationally challenged family provides a vivid metaphor for everyone. The important places in your home that are hives of activity will get an elevated status. By placing importance on those places, you drive home the idea that unnecessary and unimportant items do not need to congregate in those spaces.

The Pareto Principle or the 80/20 Rule

The Pareto Principle is a business concept that states that 80 percent of results are achieved through 20 percent of effort. The principle is named for Italian economist Vilifredo Pareto who researched Italian wealth in the late 19th century, concluding that 80 percent of the wealth in the area was owned by 20 percent of the population. In the 1940s, Joseph Juran, a management consultant extrapolated this idea and applied it to quality and efficiency issues in American businesses. Since then, the mathematic idea has simplified to an 80/20 rule.

When applied to organization in the home, the 80/20 rule can help us make decisions about our stuff. For example, when you analyze your closet, you will see that you wear 20 percent of your clothing, 80 percent of the time. Thus, 80 percent of your wardrobe is not being fully utilized and you could probably pare down some items. In my closet, I have black leggings and jeans that are worn every week, or 80 percent of the time. However, there are dress pants, leather pants and a couple pairs of crazy patterned trousers that see very little wear time, so about 20 percent or less of the time. The same idea will apply to your kitchen utensils, your toiletries, your cleaning supplies, and so on. Just by noticing that you are not using everything can help you eliminate things from your life. There is a reason that you utilize the 20 percent of your stuff. Those items are more comfortable, more convenient, or just more efficient. They are the best of your items, and you should cherish them. That does not mean that the other 80 percent are useless, but those items are taking up a lot of space and chances are that once you really dig in and look, many of those things can be tossed or donated.

The weather recently turned cold in Ohio and my husband and I were frantically searching around for hats, gloves and scarves, as you do when you are surprised with a 20 degree morning. We found items were stashed in four different places: our bedroom closet, our hall closet, our mudroom closet and in the basement. Over the past couple of winters, we were basically buying more stuff instead of taking the time to find everything and make one dedicated space for the winter gear. When we put everything together, we soon realized that we were only wearing a couple of the items. We had gloves with no matches, gloves that were chewed up by the dog in his puppy phase, hats that were too tight, scarves that were in dark depressing colors, and other pieces of clothing that were just not comfortable or flattering. My husband had one particularly hideous hat from our skiing days that was shaped like an elf cap that made me embarrassed to be seen in his vicinity. We definitely only needed 20 percent of the items. I really only like to wear my fur lined hat, my Bluetooth headphone hat or my Steelers hat; therefore, I did not need to keep any other cold weather hats, especially the fluorescent orange one or the cheetah print cap. The same thing happened with gloves and scarves; we easily pared them down to a manageable cubby. Since I went into the exercise knowing that I only wore about 20 percent of the totality, it made it easier to sort and toss items.

This idea can also be applied to your daily schedule. Basically, 20 percent of your activities results in 80 percent of your productivity, so it is a wise idea to audit your life and work smarter, not harder. But I will discuss this in the next section on scheduling.

The Creation of a Personal Oasis Approach

When cleaning and organizing the whole house is just too overwhelming, your family might want to begin with creating a personal oasis— a place that invokes peace and happiness and counteracts the clutter and chaos outside. In her book *how to keep house while drowning: a gentle approach to cleaning and organizing*, KC Davis states, "You don't exist to serve your space; your space exists to serve you" (9). In other words, don't become a slave to your household by constantly purging, organizing, and cleaning. Instead, recognize that your space is there to help you and to provide shelter and comfort. Virginia Wolfe famously states in her essay, *A Room of One's Own*, "All I could do was to offer you an opinion upon one minor point—a woman must have money and a room of her own if she is to write fiction." Thank goodness women have come a long way since 1929 and many of us now have our own rooms to think, work and create. We have added to our modern vocabulary—terms like she shed, craft room, hobby room, man cave, great room, family den, media center, game room, etc. So instead of getting bogged down on tedious things like sorting laundry and alphabetizing your spice rack, consider creating a personal oasis for each member of your family. These spaces will be given great importance for tasks like rest, self-care, work, study, and creation.

First—identify the oasis area for each person. For example, in my home, I wanted my bedroom to be my oasis with a dedicated area for me to sit and do skincare at night, a neatly organized closet and a comfortable bed with space on my bedside stand for my book, iPad and lip gloss. My husband wanted a recliner where he could access a table to do work on his computer with a television nearby. When they were younger, my daughters wanted a playroom that held all their toys but had space to spread out and build villages of Fisher Price Little People and Polly Pockets. As they got older, the family den with a big screen television, a mini refrigerator and comfy furniture became their oasis to decompress or visit with friends. Your oasis can be as simple as a corner nook where you can work on your laptop or a basement room that you can turn into a woodworking shop. Figure out what feeds your soul or helps you decompress and make that the focus of the oasis. That space will be designed and kept sacred for that task. If the workout area is your happy place, don't allow the equipment to become covered with clothing or toys. If you love cooking elaborate meals in your kitchen, don't allow bills and paperwork to cover your butcher block. If your family den is where everyone wants to veg out and rest, don't let all the furniture become covered with laundry baskets and clutter.

In her book, *From Clutter to Clarity*, organizational expert Kerri Richardson defines two types of clutter: simple and stubborn. The simple clutter is the everyday stuff that gets everywhere but is relatively easy to remove and return to its home. The stubborn clutter is the stuff that is difficult to clear. It is often hard to pinpoint the clutter and figure out where the stuff should belong. When first creating your oasis, you might need to deal with stubborn clutter. For example, if you are turning your never used dining room into a quilting area, you might need to remove all the dishes from your china cabinet so you can use it to store fabric and sewing supplies. Now you have to make a home for all of the dishes. Maybe you got the dishes for a wedding present, or the set belonged to your beloved grandmother. This is where you must keep your eyes on the prize. Envision the perfect quilting room. Find pictures in magazines or on the internet. Sketch out your vision. I bet there are no dishes or knickknacks in your vision. Pack everything up carefully and get the stuff out of your oasis. If you are a decisive person, act now. If not, put the boxes in storage and decide later if you should keep, donate, or sell. The key here is to create the oasis, the one space of tranquility and happiness. Later, you can employ other techniques to get rid of stuff or transform other rooms.

When I was turning my bedroom into a peaceful oasis, it was easy to organize my closet and streamline my cosmetics, but it was more difficult to deal with the clutter that invariably erupted on my bedside stand and on the fireplace mantle. I had to corral my husband's habit of emptying his pockets on any and all flat surfaces in the room. And I had to pare down the supplies by my bed, like different lotions, several books, socks and more. Furthermore, I soon realized that I did not want a bunch of knickknacks and decorative items around the room. In fact, pictures, vases, and plants were creating anxiety for me by their mere existence in my room. I wanted the room to be beautiful, so we put up patterned wallpaper and created nice lighting, but I wanted the room free of objects that quickly turned into clutter. This was difficult because many items in the room were important to us, like family photos and other objects. My husband is not bothered by sentimental objects, in fact, he really likes them. My solution was to free up bookcase space on our stairwell by donating old books and to create a new area for family mementos, one *outside* of my peaceful oasis and in an area that was accessible to the whole family.

Once you have created the oasis and taken the time to make it beautiful and remove the stubborn clutter, you need to find a way to stay on top of the upkeep and maintenance of your peaceful space. For example, stay on top of the simple clutter of items that try to creep into your oasis like paperwork, toys, laundry, and other items. Also, make sure your oasis stays relevant. After all— your crafting room is a space to actively make crafts, not just a storage area for craft supplies. If you lose joy in woodworking, then sell or donate your tools and create a new oasis for another passion project that feeds your soul. It is okay to change your mind and to grow into new projects. After all, our kids grow up and no longer need nurseries and playrooms; we adults grow and change our hobbies and passion projects as well.

Health issues and aging might also prompt you to create a new oasis. If you or a loved one is confined to a smaller area, then this is when you want to focus your energies on making that one area something special. Surround them with their sentimental objects if that is their desire or clean out everything and make the place airy and bright. Your approach will depend on individual preferences and health needs. If you need space for medical equipment and personnel, then you don't want to have it full of tripping and clutter hazards.

The nice thing about the oasis approach is that it provides a space that is free of the stress of clutter and objects that just don't belong in the area. When you make the decision to create just ONE nice room or space, it is easy to move out all the other objects that do not fit the overall vision. Sure, those items might now clutter up your basement, living room or attic, but at least they will be out of sight in your most important spaces of the home. This method also provides you with a retreat. For those of you who deal with collectors, procrastinators and messy people, this retreat can be your personal space that stays off limits to everyone else's stuff. This will take constant redirection, and you will have to set clear boundaries.

When my children were young, my office was in an attic alcove. The rest of the attic was the children's playroom. I had a wonderful woman named Wava who came to the house and played with the children several days a week when I really had to get work done, but as an entrepreneur, I often had to do work in small bursts to keep projects going or check on things. I loved hearing the kids playing and being right beside me, but their toys, papers, dishes, socks and more would start migrating into my office space. Our solution was to hang clear French doors at the alcove entrance. I could see my kids running around, but the door was a clear reminder that mom's workspace was off limits for clutter. It was also a great reminder for the kids and their friends to NOT come in to borrow markers, pens, or papers and mess up my work stuff. After all, they had their own office area with desks and craft supplies located on the other end of the attic. However, even the doors were not a big enough boundary. I remember one particular summer when the kids and their friends were on school vacation and often at our house. The kids really got into a craft project and kept going in and out of my office to use my work supplies. We went on a shopping trip to beef up their supplies, but the kids kept coming in and out of the office. I soon realized that it wasn't my stuff—but the allure of mom's workspace that was driving these constant disturbances. I didn't mind the kids using my stapler, but I did mind having all their friends coming in and poking around my spreadsheets and projects. That is when we held a family meeting about personal privacy and boundaries. After all, the kids didn't want me to go into their rooms and read their diaries or scroll through all their text messages. They got the idea quickly. I hung up a nice sign that basically said no trespassing in my office or else and that helped keep the nosy friends from coming in and out.

Since my husband has semi-retired, he is home more often than I am used to. Because I work from home, I was not prepared for the disruption that one grown man can inflict, like asking me "What are you doing?" (Umm, working, like I do every day—in complete silence, preferably.) or "Where are the double A batteries?" (In the kitchen drawer where they have lived comfortably for the last 25 years.) To co-exist in this new normal, we had to establish some parameters and set up some separate work areas. The main problem here is that my work area oasis has a cozy fireplace and a television. For the past several years, I worked alone in this oasis during the day, but Todd would come see me there in the evenings when we would watch a show together while I worked on a craft project, or he checked emails. It was a great space because it was far from the kitchen so kept us on track diet-wise and very cozy, especially in the winter. Since Todd worked very long hours, I got plenty of time in my oasis. Once he started working at home on his medical software business, things got tricky. I did NOT want to share my oasis since it was where I was most productive and comfortable. Todd was used to working with lots of people around him, so he didn't understand my need to work alone. He thought it would be fine for him to work in the same area. To resolve this tricky issue, I asked Todd to visualize his perfect workspace. It turns out that he wanted a huge, curved monitor to set up along with his laptop to work from a command center of sorts. And it turns out that this command center would not fit in the current office oasis (convenient for me, right?!). He also wanted a big table to spread out all his current projects, like cataloguing coins and signing patient medical records. Long story short, we realized we rarely used our dining room—as in once or twice per year (Thanksgiving and Christmas), and it was a very warm room in the winter. So, we set up his command center in the dining room and learned to schedule times in the attic oasis when we could both work on something. I learned to schedule my busy work that didn't require a lot of brain power for the times when Todd wanted to enjoy the cozy attic as well.

The key here is that it is okay for you to have a retreat or as Virginia Woolf says, "a room of one's own." Every human in your house deserves an area for reflection and retreat, whether it be a bedroom, an alcove, a nook or even a special chair. Everyone at my house knows that the recliner in the attic is Daddy's chair. He loves the space so much since it gives him a great view of the television and lets him put his feet up when he is tired. And my oldest child has proclaimed the right end of the couch in the living room as her "spot." Even though Maddie is now 27 years old and has her own house, we still abide by that rule and defer to her when she comes home! Not everyone will have the luxury of carving out an entire room, but by working together, your family can visualize and vocalize the needs for an oasis—even if it is a shared space like a kitchen or living room. Make that room sacred with no unwanted clutter or objects that belong to other parts of the home. Inspire everyone to do a quick five-minute pick up at the end of each day so that the area stays on point. If you just have one tranquil spot, the rest of the household chaos and clutter will be more manageable and less stressful overall. And who knows, if you carve out the one family oasis, everyone might be motivated to move on to cleaning up the other areas of the home.

The Hand Holding or Companionship Approach

It's just a fact of life that some people need more help than others. There is a fine line, of course, between helping and enabling. I do NOT advocate doing things FOR people all the time. However, being present and helping someone out is perfectly fine! The helper can be a friend, a family member or even a paid person. The key here is for the companion to provide support to someone while he or she cleans and organizes the space.

Sometimes just thinking that someone will come over is the impetus your family member will need to get motivated. My daughter Isabelle will tell her ADHD friend Emily that she is coming to visit just to get Emily motivated to clean her apartment. I was skeptical that this ruse would work, but Isabelle assures me that in her ADHD crowd, this is a helpful method! In any case, I think that having a companion is another valid approach, especially for people who need assistance with focus and staying on task.

A good way for the helper to start is with the question, "What do you want to get out of this organizing session?" That question immediately provides focus and makes your organizationally-challenged person visualize and vocalize the goal. Most importantly, the companion must remember that he or she is the nonjudgmental third party in the room. In other words, gentle prompts and assistance are good, but making decisions for the other person is counterproductive and won't help in the long run.

My husband is the prime example of someone who loves a hand holder. Since I live intimately with him, I am really too close to be his hand holder in this situation. I just want to be able to walk through my bedroom without seeing his clutter everywhere, and I want it taken care of swiftly. Todd, however, needs to really consider everything and have someone there to keep him on task. He is notorious for pulling everything out to sort and then walking away from said pile to start another task. He needs someone to constantly prompt him to finish that task before starting another one. I am too impatient and irritated to fulfill that role! Thus, we need that third party bystander to come in and provide a nonjudgmental viewpoint. We have hired a great person, Cyndi, who is this excellent buffer. She is a really organized person, so she knows what needs to be done. Also, she is patient and kind with Todd because she doesn't have to live with him! It is a win-win situation. I get the payoff of a nice clean house, and Todd gets his stuff sorted without feeling alone and unfocused. Again, if you have the financial means, consider outsourcing tasks that are particularly difficult for your family. Hiring Cyndi, for us, is way cheaper than marriage counseling and we get a clean house in the end!

Accountability is a great tool to use in the completion of many tasks. When you have a walking buddy waiting on you in the morning, you are more likely to get out of bed and do that morning exercise. And if you pay someone to come help you, then you are more likely to follow through on the task you need to complete. You will be less likely to come up with an excuse to avoid the task. For example, I have a friend who pays for a personal trainer to meet her at the gym. My friend knows that the simple act of scheduling and paying the trainer, motivates her to show up and to work out more vigorously than if she showed up alone.

I have found that all my daughters like some sort of companionship when going through their stuff as well. While Isabelle might need more direct help and prompts, the other two just like having me or another friend in the room to chat with while they empty out drawers and refold clothing. Therefore, make sure you consider your family members and their need for companionship. Some might need an active participant who will prompt them and keep them on task, while others just don't want to be alone when they are doing such a boring task.

When we cleaned out my husband's clothing, his suits and dinner jackets were taking up a huge hunk of his closet. Since he was now semi-retired and attended professional meetings less often, Todd did not need all the suits and jackets he had acquired over the past couple of decades. And many, I knew, were completely out of date or did not fit. I had already had someone help me take everything out of his closet, so I carried these all downstairs over a weekend when our adult children were in town. Todd then put on a fashion show with a couple of daughters and a son-in-law to give him their valuable input. Todd did not want to do this task alone and it would never have been completed unless we made it into a fun party. Having companions to interact with him made it a much more enjoyable experience, and we all liked making fun of some of the more dubious jackets and giving him some compliments on ones that he needed to pull out more often for dinners and events. Todd also appreciated getting some advice on what was in fashion. We hadn't gone out much during the pandemic so were unaware of the new trends. This allowed him to figure out some new color combinations he could try out. When we went out to dinner with friends and they complimented Todd on his stellar outfit, that solidified the value of having companions to help him with his wardrobe decisions.

If you are having a hard time finishing a task, your helper can also come in and save the day. When my youngest daughter was moving from Ohio to Colorado to attend college, it took weeks for us to figure out what stuff we were going to pack into three suitcases that weighed under 50 pounds. Isabelle did a big clean up of her closet and started pulling out stuff that she wanted to take for the three years that she would be living in Colorado. She made piles of clothing and shoes all over the room, but we were both having a block when it came time to complete the suitcases. I was sad about her leaving, and Isabelle was having difficulty figuring out how to get everything contained in the three cases. When our good friend Caroline heard about our dilemma, she offered her expert service. Caroline travels often and all over the world, so she was well versed in how to best pack a suitcase. She asked us to go and finish up some of our last-minute errands in town and then Caroline "finished the puzzle" of packing three suitcases. If someone in your home is having trouble just completing an important task, friends and other family members are great resources to provide an expert opinion or to use their expertise to help you get over that finish line.

Your third-party bystander can be a proactive helper by performing these types of tasks:
- Helping you sort items into piles.
- Helping you find where the items should be located. Do they stay in that room, or should they relocate to another part of the house?

- Helping you hang or fold and put away clothing.
- Providing independent reviews on what clothing looks good on you or which shoes look worn out and dated.
- Helping you stay on task with prompts like, "Let's finish this pile before we move to the next area," or "What do we need to do to finish organizing this cupboard?"
- Providing you with entertainment and companionship while you perform boring tasks like sorting all your socks or emptying out drawers in your craft room.
- Helping you fully complete your task at hand, so you don't have further clutter or chaos to deal with later.
- Helping you be accountable to show up and complete your goals.
- Helping you cross that finish line and complete important tasks.

The Tackle the Scary First Approach

While some families need to start with small, fun organizational projects like cleaning out drawers and closets, others need to go right to the final battle and take on the monster of the house—like the unruly basement or completely jumbled up garage. These are your adrenaline junkies who prefer to have a big win and brag about the victory.

One neighbor family of mine had a garage that was packed to the gills with everything from bicycles and camping gear to lawn equipment and broken furniture. The parents had a vision of finally being able to park their cars in the garage and were determined to make that happen before winter. Their teenage son, Jay, had just learned to drive, so he was on board with the vision. Since his parents worked at the same company, Jay was getting to drive one of the cars to school every day, and he preferred to get into a warm car with no frost on the window for those 6:30 am mornings in January. Jay's mom, Marie, confided in me that since her two older daughters had gone off to college, she had a lot of decluttering and organizing to do in the house, but her son and husband were not interested in helping with those tasks. However, they were interested in the cars and all the lawn maintenance and athletic gear items, so they were willing to tackle the garage—a project that Marie found completely overwhelming and uninteresting since none of the stuff belonged to her.

Taking advantage of their interest, Marie scheduled a nice balmy September weekend to pull everything out of the garage and tackle the monster to the ground. Once everything was out, she and her husband purchased a small shed from the local hardware store and her son filled it with all the gardening tools and lawn mowing equipment that they deemed functional and worthy of keeping. Then while the men sorted through athletic equipment and camping gear, Marie swept and painted the garage. While sorting through everything, Marie's husband found the hooks and organizational systems that he had purchased twenty years ago when they first moved into the house. Utilizing these found treasures, he and Jay spent the Sunday finding and preparing wall space to hang the bicycles and camping gear that they wanted to keep.

Since Marie was more invested in the interior spaces of her home, she would have never thought about tackling the scary garage. She didn't do lawn work and could care less about camping and biking. There were tools, chemicals and auto parts strewn everywhere. She would not have known what needed to be kept or what was worthy of selling or donating. Truth be told, she would have just thrown everything away or just left the chaotic, messy room locked away from her daily vision.

While she initially would have preferred that her husband and son help her with sorting through and organizing things in the house, Marie saw that the garage operation was a monumental win for her two men. They both found things that they had been looking for or had forgotten that they already owned. Furthermore, they were now well poised to do lawncare and automobile maintenance with everything neatly arranged and labeled. And finally, the broken furniture and old sports equipment were removed so that the cars could have the valuable, heated real estate. And since Marie provided some impressive ancillary support in picking out a garden shed, cleaning the garage, and painting the walls, the men could do the hard labor of removing all the heavy items and doing the big sort that needed to occur. And when the neighbors all came over to ooh and ah at the huge transformation that happened within one weekend, the family members all felt pride in their accomplishment. The job was such a success that Marie got the guys to agree to another big project, tackling the basement storage area so that they could make it into a family den with a new, big television for watching football games and movies. Marie realized that these two family members were only interested in large scale projects with huge payoffs. Once she harnessed that energy and encouraged them to move forth, she became more inclined to do her own, smaller scale organization projects that gave her joy and peace within the home.

My sister-in-law calls the scary part of her house that gets cluttered quickly, her "doom room." This is the place where everyone kicks off shoes, where laundry gets piled, where the mail is partially opened and then abandoned, where craft projects are started but not finished, where someone dumped out a drawer to look for something and left everything in a pile on the floor and where clutter just seemingly multiplies overnight. The doom room is an ongoing problem that will not be resolved until you take action and put into place some rules for everyone in the house. You can definitely schedule a full-on attack of the room and get everything situated, but if it is a high traffic area, it will go back to full on clutter unless you put into place a daily routine which we will discuss later in the chapter.

The First Responder Approach

Often in war, military leaders send in an initial wave of troops, often ground troops, to pave the way for a more knowledgeable, larger scale operation. While I don't normally advocate fully organizing for other people, there is an approach that can work here. This works best when the person is not emotionally attached to the items and is not a collector or sentimental soul. This also can work on an operation that involves number six above, like tackling a scary basement or garage.

For this approach, you send in a first responder to assess the situation and provide you with some much-needed muscle work, cleaning, maintenance work or assessment help. For example, you might hire a couple of strong individuals to remove everything from your attic or basement so that you can swoop in and do the sorting and organizing. You might have the same team shop vac the area or refresh the walls with paint so that you can be more motivated to sort and organize. If your team is knowledgeable about the items in your space, you can even ask them to do some preliminary sorting.

For example, I had a couple of housekeepers for my business that were looking for some extra work. My closet space is in a turret-style room with windows and had not been cleaned in years. I asked them to spend a few hours removing everything from the closet, completely dusting and cleaning all the surfaces. Since they are fashionable women, I asked them to look over my items before they put them back and to make a pile of things that they thought were dated or worn. No one had ever asked them to do that type of work, so I think they were initially reluctant and afraid they might insult me with their choices. Once I reassured them that I would not be hurt and to just do their best, they tackled the task easily. I came home from work that day to piles of things they deemed to be unfashionable or too scruffy to wear. And you know what? They were right. There were at least 8 pairs of shoes that were way too scuffed to wear in public, let alone donate. I kept one pair of flip flops to just walk to my neighbor's pool and the rest were tossed. When I looked through the dresses and shirts they pulled out, I was surprised at some of the choices at first, but when I thought about it, they were right. They were items that were pretty colors and that I had worn a lot in the past, but they were no longer relevant or fashionable and I hadn't worn them in a while. Their unbiased assessment helped me better evaluate the items in my closet.

Having that first responder team come in first is also a great way to get motivated to tackle an organizational task. If your family members trust you as the expert, you might even perform this task, allowing the other family members to arrive partway through the process to better sort and provide input about how things should be arranged or put away. This worked well when we got to my husband's part of the closet. I knew my cleaning ladies did not want to make decisions about Todd's clothing. So, I asked them to keep everything out of his closet on my bed. I then went through everything. Things that I knew fit him and that he wore often, I simply put back in the closet, arranging pants into two categories: dress pants and casual pants and putting short-sleeve shirts separate from long-sleeved ones. Then I assessed the rest of his clothing, putting some more into the closet and then putting stained, worn ones in one pile and unfashionable ones in another. Thus, when Todd came home from work, he was able to look at those two piles and give me his input. When he agreed with my decision, I put those items in the trash or in a donation bag. The rest of the shirts and pants got hung back in the closet. Todd would never have gone through his wardrobe; it is just not an important or high stress area for him. Having some workers clean first, then having me sort was a big help to the process. We laid the groundwork, and he came in and made the tactical decisions.

If you have ever watched any home organization shows, then you know that the television producers and hosts send in a team of workers to pull everything out of the home space and place it on tarps in the front yard so the homeowners can look at everything and make decisions. This works well for everyone, but especially for people with ADHD who have a difficult time when things are hidden away in closets, boxes, drawers, and bookcases. They need to see all the options put together in one place before their brains can start to focus on which items can stay and which items can be removed.

The Embrace the Clutter Approach

Okay, I know, this one is going to sound a little odd and antithetical in creating a nicely uncluttered home, but bear with me. This approach will mostly apply to the collector personalities in your home. They have a lot of stuff that they find sentimental, interesting, or just plain cool. You might look at all of it and say that it is all pure trash. But your collecting family members see treasure and they will accuse you of not seeing their vision. Everyone deserves to have some fun in life and for the sentimental souls, collecting is their hobby and their joy. If you are lucky, there is just one main collection to deal with, like Beanie Babies, coins, or angel statues. If this is the case, you and your collector just need to find an area where the items can be displayed and visually enjoyed. If there are too many items, maybe you can negotiate a system where some items are displayed and others are stored and rotated in and out, kind of like a museum display. This is also where you can negotiate your personal oasis as a clutter free zone to counteract the display section for your collector.

If you are not lucky and your loved one is moving towards extreme collecting or hoarding, then you will need to consider some other options. If hoarding is the issue, then you need to seek mental health assistance and therapy to try to work towards resolution. If, however, you are just dealing with someone who really enjoys stuff and wants to keep it organized and nice, then you will need to have some discussions about how to move forward to keep the house from becoming too full and chaotic.

Here are some questions to ask your sentimental souls:

- **What collections do you need to keep?**

   Extreme collectors tend to have multiple collections that they have developed over the years. However, like anyone else, they may have outgrown the collection or focused the collection onto a specific niche or quality. For example, my daughter really enjoyed owls as a child, probably because of the Harry Potter novels and movies where the children received mail delivered by majestic owls. Therefore, she started collecting owls and we all started buying her cute owl things. Now, Maddie is 27 years old and while she still loves the Harry Potter novels, she has moved beyond her dream of being a student at Hogwarts. She has developed other hobbies like making craft cocktails and playing with her cats. She just purchased her first home with her husband and the owl collection didn't make the decorative cut. However, she still thinks owls are cute and she knows that her family members loved buying these items for her. She had to give permission to herself to get rid of the bulk of the collection, only keeping some practical items like potholders and owl sheets.

   It is worth asking your collector if he or she has outgrown or lost interest in some collections. It is also worth asking if some items from collections could be removed. For example, my husband is a coin collector. Over the years Todd has collected a bunch of different coins that he just liked; he also acquired some full collections from other family members who passed away. In the beginning, Todd liked all the coins he came across. But he soon realized that he had to narrow down his focus, so he spent a decade or so just concentrating on and off on only American coins. Now he is in a semi-retired phase of life where he wants to fine tune his collection to just a couple of different types of coins that he really enjoys—like large cents and half dollars—and concentrate his efforts on finding the best examples to complete these collections.

In order to refine his collection, Todd sold all the other coins on eBay, using the proceeds to only buy coins in his two categories.

- **What is the overall goal for your collection?**

  This is where you want your collector to really look at the collection and vocalize the overall goal. Is it to possess as many dolls as she can or is it to have just one type of each American Girl Doll? Try to get your collectors to think in terms of a museum collection where you carefully curate each item. When a doll in better condition is found, you sell the other doll that is not as good. You don't keep both dolls. Tell your collector that the money from sold items go towards new things that are better or for better storage or display for the items.

- **Are there any collections that can be sold or passed along to another family member?**

  For my daughter Maddie, it was easy for her to just donate the extra owls that she no longer wanted. For my husband, the extra coins became a sales opportunity where he could sell the collections he no longer wanted and use the money to purchase coins for the two categories that he decided to keep. This is also a chance to see if anyone in the family is interested in your collection and to give that person their inheritance now. This is a great idea, since you ensure that the collection goes to the person you designate, instead of taking the gamble that after death that inheritance wish will be honored. If you decide to donate or sell a collection, some of your family members may just want one or two items for sentimental reasons. When I decided to sell all my Smurf mugs from the 1980s, my kids each took one mug to keep in their kitchens. They remembered these cups from childhood and keeping one mug was enough to just keep that fun memory alive.

- **Is there a space where the items can be displayed in the home?**

    This goes back to the idea of creating a personal oasis. Your collector will most likely want a nice bookshelf or wall display case to contain their items and put them on display. This is a good time to find a room or area to make this dream come alive. If your kids are small or you have older family members currently inhabiting your home, you may just earmark an area to use in the future when those rooms become available. The key here is to have a plan so that the collection does not take over other rooms and create chaos. If your collector knows that he or she gets that area when your youngest child finishes graduate school, then he or she is more likely to keep the collection in one area until it can be lovingly displayed.

- **What types of display cases or containers would help you organize your collection?**

    This is an area you do NOT want to rush into. I have made the mistake of encouraging my husband to buy lots of different containers for his items, only to find out that the containers were not practical or adequate. Instead, get the entire collection out in one place where you can see all the items and brainstorm together how to best contain or display the items. Maybe you want to hire someone to build a lighted cabinet or maybe you can repurpose a dining room cabinet that you never utilize. You might want to remove the books from your shelves and instead use that area to display your pottery collection for all to see.

    My husband has always had the dream of displaying his Atari game cartridge collection. After getting out the consols and setting them up to play games with our daughters, Todd realized that no one wanted to play these vintage games for more than five minutes. The graphics and gameplay just cannot compete with the PlayStation we have in our family living room. I suggested that he catalogue his collection because all I could see were several large plastic containers piling up in the basement. When we put out all the games in one place, even Todd was shocked at how many he had and how many multiple copies he owned. He had at least 30 copies of Space Invaders alone. For the next step, he entered them all into a spreadsheet. He is in the current process of finding the best copy of each game so that the rest can be sold. Then he will be able to stack the games in wooden shelf displays in the basement which will look really cool and will be an improvement over just looking at 18 plastic tubs stacked against the wall.

- **Can we afford to buy or rent another space, off property, where these items can be organized, displayed, and stored?**

I'm not really in favor of renting out a storage unit just to hold stuff, but if you can afford it, this is preferable to having a house of chaos and clutter. I would only do this rental for specific, organized collections that have a purpose or interest for someone in your household. Also, I would ensure that the storage unit gets reviewed on a quarterly basis, or at the minimum, yearly. We have all seen television shows and TikTok videos where people go to look at their storage units and are shocked at the items that they kept and have been paying for monthly. Before taking this step—think outside the box. Is there another area where these items can be stored or displayed that will not hamper your space? For example, do you have understanding in-laws who will allow their basement to become the new storage area? Do you have the funds to purchase a property where the items can live permanently? The key here is that a separate area for storage is worth it—if it keeps clutter and mayhem from your family home.

For example, my husband and I own rental properties. We were able to allocate a property where he can triage his items: pull them out, look through them, organize them and sell or donate them. This is the perfect system for us. I do not have to look at the items or have them in my way on a daily basis. And Todd has an area of his own where he can enjoy his hobby. In fact, during the COVID pandemic, Todd spent several months in his private storage area, creating a speakeasy. Utilizing antiques that he collected over the years, he took a large basement room and divided it into four smaller rooms with seating areas, mood lighting and collection displays. He repurposed an antique organ and turned it into a bar. He had collected a variety of bookcases, cabinets and shelves over the years and used them to divide rooms and hold glassware. We had furniture that we had rotated out of our house and an old iron bathtub that we took out of a rental unit and turned into a sofa. Since he had a fascination with old luggage that he got cheap at yard sales and flea markets, Todd had the perfect items to create a hinged, false wall that became the entrance to the speakeasy.

Once the pandemic ended, we held a party for our friends, not telling them anything, but just sending out invitations with a secret entry password. I think this was the first time that all of us could see Todd's genius. Everyone knew he liked stuff and we all made fun of him for years. But we could not see his vision. Collectors do have a method to their madness, and many can create treasure from trash. However, without space and time, your collectors cannot make these visions reality. As the organized (and sane) one, you can help them find that area and still protect the sanctity of your family home.

- **Do you have a stopping point for your different collections?**

When dealing with extreme collectors, this is a crucial question. After all, you cannot collect EVERYTHING. And your funds and space might present some realistic obstacles to extreme collecting. Once my husband created his new speakeasy, he was able to get rid of some furniture that didn't make the cut in his creation. Since he could not find a reason to keep some items, he was amenable to me posting to Facebook marketplace and unloading those things. Therefore, it is important to go through all these collection questions and help your collector review the entire collection and plan for its future. Going through these questions will help your collector see how to improve the collection process, to refine and hone the collection and to get rid of items that are taking away from the overall vision.

The good thing is that many collectors are motivated by a sense of accomplishment that comes through completing a collection. Utilize this urge for completion to motivate your collector to stay focused and to get rid of items that distract from the main goal. Your collector is proud of his or her collection, so use that sense of pride as well! Point out the ways in which you can display a focused or carefully curated collection. Your collector might then start to see the items which are detracting from the overall collection and that can be permanently eliminated.

My husband was motivated through the process to sell a lot of items. We started selling things on social media and eBay and held a couple of yard sales. As we started making money on these items, Todd had to curb his desire to acquire more stuff. Just because we were getting rid of items did not mean that we were open to bringing in more items.

Your collectors probably enjoy going to auctions, yard sales, thrift stores and flea markets. They are going to have to curb their desire to purchase more items again and again. By clearly defining and writing down their collections, they will be more mindful of the overall vision. Another way to help the collectors on these shopping sprees is to go with them or ask them to send you pictures while at the sale. My husband was in the habit of buying things that he thought I would want or that I could use in the home. However, he didn't know that I already had a quality pan that size or that I only liked cloth tablecloths that would not need to be ironed. He saw a good deal and his love language meant that he wanted to present me with a gift. However, the overall process works best when he shows me the items so I can choose. Sometimes Todd really hits a homerun, like the time he found me a brand-new Dyson vacuum at the auction for just $50. Praise your collectors for their good finds so they are encouraged to involve you in the process of finding things that fit your home well.

The Little and Often Approach

Having a daily routine is a great organizational tool but often out of reach for your procrastinators and ADHD family members. After all, these are the same people who have difficulty in breaking down tasks into small pieces. I was hard on my youngest daughter until I realized how she saw the world in her ADHD consciousness. She was excellent at dealing with high stress situations. She went through intense cancer treatments amazingly because she could deal with rapid change and impulsivity. However, she could not manage her four-times-a-day medicine regime, so that was something that had to be outsourced to me and other family members because it was too important to not fulfill. Also, day-to-day routines were paralyzing for Isabelle because when she tried to get ready in the morning, she might be on the way to take a shower but then realize that she needed to find a particular shirt to wear and once she was digging through laundry to find it, she might realize that she never switched the clothes from the washer to the dryer so then she has to do that task and on the way there she realizes that she did her homework in the attic so needs to go retrieve it to put in her backpack which is in her car so she goes out there and realizes that she only has ten minutes to get ready to leave for school. It's a circle that gets repeated every day. (This must be why she loved the book, *If You Give a Mouse a Cookie* as a child because that mouse gets waylaid at every new event.) For those with ADHD, this circular rhythm occurs daily and contributes to mounting frustration and the desire to just give up trying to be organized and on time.

To succeed, Isabelle had to enlist help in figuring out how to break down her tasks into smaller portions and in getting prompts to get her back on track. Medication, of course, helped, but we still needed strategies that made sense to her. A little and often technique with phone reminders and timers became a go-to system for her when approaching homework and household tasks. So that she does not become too absorbed in a task, Isabelle must set a timer to remind her to quit and go on to something else. For example, Isabelle might get a burst of energy and want to clean her apartment, but then she gets so caught up in that cleaning that she neglects to do the homework that is due to her professor that evening.

When faced with staying organized and clutter-free, Isabelle often has the same all or nothing outlook. She will either organize to the point of not doing important schoolwork and appointments or she will do nothing and let everything pile up. Thus, what works for her is a little and often approach, where she makes lists of tasks with reminders and checks them off. She can put constant issues, like laundry and organizing school papers on a repetition rotation with reminders on her phone or on a list on her whiteboard. In her book, *Self-Care for People with ADHD*, Sasha Hamdani advocates a method of decluttering where you just pick up 13 items. You don't just do one or two which will make no difference to the daily mess, but you don't tackle the whole project and lose the rest of your day. Thirteen items is significant enough to make a difference but not all-encompassing for ADHD people who have a hard time doing things incrementally.

For some people, it makes sense to work at things a little bit at a time daily because big tasks are too overwhelming or too distracting. My neighbor Marie preferred to work on her house tasks a little bit at a time, but her son and husband wanted to do a big task all at once and see a big result. Isabelle also likes big results and will take on a huge task that distracts her from what she should really be doing, like schoolwork. To get into the groove of daily tasks, a to-do list or planner where you write down daily and weekly goals is paramount to your success. This is where some of the smart phone applications and prompting software can be of assistance.

For those of us who are more old-school, a breakdown list can be helpful. When it is my turn to host a big event like Thanksgiving for twenty people, I make a good list a couple of weeks before the event where I write down everything that I can think of that needs to occur before and during the big day. I will keep lists of ingredients, steps for recipes and a listing of tasks that need done. For example, this year about half of the guests were staying for the weekend, so my before-Thanksgiving list read like this:

- Change sheets on guest bedrooms.
- Make sure toothpaste and toiletries are in all the bathrooms.
- Set up tables and chairs in the living room.
- Put tablecloths and napkins on all the tables.
- Set tables with glassware, pitchers, plates, and silverware.
- Make quiches and breakfast casseroles and freeze.
- Make soup in a crockpot to serve the day after Thanksgiving.
- Thaw and brine turkey.
- Gather supplies for Christmas card decorating on Friday: glue guns, cardstock, vintage postcards, scissors, markers, and pens.
- Stock up on pop and wine.
- Gather supplies to make signature drinks and punch for the kids.
- Vacuum and mop all floors downstairs.

You get the idea. By breaking up a monumental task into parts, I achieve a couple of things. I ease my anxiety and worry, and I gain control and confidence. And each day for the next couple of weeks, I plug away at the tasks or outsource them where I can to my husband or other helpers.

In addition to making a great list for achieving big tasks, you can commit your family members to doing one small task each day that will help tame the overall chaos of the home. This incremental approach is great for people who are extra busy or easily overwhelmed. You are still making progress, just at a slower pace. It will take a while to see the payoff, but you might put into place a pattern that is more sustainable over time. It is kind of like dieting to lose weight. Sure, you can go on a diet medication and lose 15 pounds quickly. However, your failure rate is high since you have not changed your overall lifestyle and pattern of eating and exercising. Conversely, if you start making incremental changes in the types and quantity of food you eat and start slowly adding walking or other exercise to your routine, it will take longer to lose those 15 pounds. It might even take a full year, but by the end of that year, you will have established a clear pattern to better health and weight, and it will be more sustainable because you made small changes every day and kept up your routine.

One severely scattered person I know has two rules for herself. First, she makes her bed every day. Her house could be falling around her, but she still makes her bed. At night, she is happy in her personal haven to have a controlled area that allows her to get much needed rest. Her second rule is to de-clutter her kitchen before she goes to the grocery store. If she brings groceries to a messy kitchen, she never seems to get everything put away. Having a couple of non-negotiable tasks can be key to keeping you centered in your daily life.

For example, you may have come across the website FlyLady.net started by Marla Cilley, an organizational and cleaning guru who has also written some books about her method for keeping your house tidy. Her system is all based on creating 15 minute or less increments for household tasks. She also advocates starting a routine with some non-negotiable tasks, like cleaning your kitchen sink. Cilley maintains that keeping some set, daily standards, like having a shiny kitchen sink, will make your other tasks seem more manageable and more easily able to fit into your busy day.

Small tasks do add up and taking this approach helps your organizationally challenged family members start to set good habits and routines. In a study published in the *European Journal of Social Psychology* in 2009, researchers determined that starting a good habit took anywhere from 18 to 254 days to become part of your daily routine. The average time, overall, was 66 days to form a new habit. The variability comes from the habit or task itself. It is way easier to add a habit like drinking a glass of water at lunch everyday than to add the task of doing 30 push-ups each night before bed. However, what this study tells us overall, is that change is possible over time. Starting with small tasks and asking your family and yourself to perform them regularly will make a difference. You can change the toxic organizational culture of your home, even with extreme procrastinators and collectors; you simply need to find a way to motivate everyone to do a set of small steps day after day.

I know that this is easier said than done, but here are some ways to try to establish daily routine and motivation in your household:

- **Model the behavior yourself.** If you want your family members to try something new, then you must show them how it is done. Make a daily list for yourself of tasks that you want to complete every day and then start following the list diligently. Be vocal about your successes in adding in some tasks like doing daily squats and emptying the dishwasher. When you exhibit pride in the fact that you can keep up with these daily challenges, you will start to have an impact on others in your household.

- **Challenge your family members to take on some incremental tasks.** If you have children, then you can make these tasks the chores that they perform at the house. For your spouse or other adults, that will not work; I don't think they will appreciate you assigning them chores! Instead, ask them to take on the challenge with you of getting the house together, with small steps every day. Then you can come up with lists together to help each other stay on task and hit your goals.

- **Tame the "doom room" with daily decluttering.** Make it a rule that before bed, everyone must carry up their own stuff to their rooms or to the place where said stuff belongs. Make this non-negotiable. You can even provide everyone with a basket to go around and put all the clutter in to make the task easier. If you let a few days slide by, that clutter will multiply into an unreasonable and unmanageable problem. Keep everyone accountable or create a rotating list where everyone takes a turn decluttering your high traffic areas.

- **Establish homes for your things.** This is particularly important for your ADHD people and kept coming up in my interviews with those on that ADHD spectrum. Everyone noted that it was crucial for their room's order to have set places for items. And when multiple people are living together, it's important to take a hard look at habits. If items are easy to put away and are easily accessible when needed, then your organizational efforts will work and make life easier for everyone.

- **Post the tasks where everyone can see them.** Put up a whiteboard or chalkboard of everyone's daily incremental tasks in the kitchen so that everyone can see the information. This is especially helpful for your visual learners and those who are forgetful or unfocused.

- **Take inventory of your stuff.** It is so easy to NOT know what you already own. We waste an incredible amount of time and money in replacing items that already exist in our homes. If you are like me, you have been at the grocery store wondering if you already have mustard and enough chocolate chips to make cookies. You buy the items, only to come home to two other mustards in the pantry and a full bag of chocolate chips. When the kids were little and I was running among work, home, and school activities, this wasteful practice happened on a too often basis. Usually, I ended up donating a lot of extra pantry items at the annual food drives in town.

In my home, we also make mistakes with over purchasing clothing, household items, cleaners, and collectibles. Financial consultants working with people on saving money often urge their clients to take inventory of items before heading out the door to go shopping. Once I started taking the time to create lists of what I already own, I greatly streamlined our shopping trips and kept our home free of too many duplicated items. This inventory system works great for your collectors and keeps them from buying items already in their collection. Make sure you encourage them to create a database or pay someone to help them log all their items. This inventory is also great for insurance reasons if the collection is valuable.

Once your family members clean out wardrobes and drawers, it will become apparent what clothing items are overrepresented and can be eliminated. This will also ensure that you don't buy another pair of jeans when you already own 12 great pairs. I also use the inventory approach in many other areas of keeping my home organized. For example, I keep an inventory sheet in the drawer of our kitchen to indicate what alcohol bottles are in our cupboard bar. Then before a party I don't have to guess whether we have vodka or gin. My inventory sheet tells me what bottles are in the bar and what are in reserve for future use. I also keep a notebook paper in my freezer with all the items I have in frozen storage. Then I can easily check it to see if I have a dessert frozen or a casserole that I can defrost for dinner. This is especially helpful during the holidays when we are preparing in advance for visits and events. The inventory sheet will tell me that I have two rum cakes, a breakfast quiche and three dozen cookies ready for action. You could also do this for your pantry, your household cleaners, your junk drawer in the kitchen and your party supplies. No longer will you have to guess what items are readily available. I like the approach of putting notebook papers in each spot to review; however, you might find it a better practice to keep these lists in one journal, in your calendar or in your smartphone.

- **Be realistic about what tasks can be completed on a daily or weekly basis in an incremental fashion.** You want to impress upon your family members the fact that they should not make promises that cannot be kept. For example, I'm not a morning person, so making the daily goal to get up and walk every day at 6:00 am is not realistically going to happen. Some of your family members will over-promise simply because they do not want to disappoint you. That is just setting up everyone for failure from the start. This is where you, as the organizational guru of the household, can step in and help your person make a more realistic list. Start small. Just getting two tasks done in a regular fashion will make a huge impact over time. There is no need to conquer the world all at once.

- **Consider creating a reward system for completion.** Once you make new habit goals, it is a good idea to tie your efforts to a reward. This is particularly easy when the kids are young, and you create a chore chart with stickers to keep them motivated and into the routine. For your ADHD people and adults, this is probably not going to work. Instead, tell your ADHD messy kid that if he or she keeps their room picked up for the next two months, you will reward them with some item that they have been wanting to purchase. The key here is to get to that 66-day mark when the good habit is more likely to stick. If lack of motivation affects your significant other, talk to him or her about trying to meet that same goal of 66 days with a series of organizational tasks. In fact, you can both set goals to meet. If you are already organized and on task, pick another goal that is difficult for you, like sticking to regular exercise. Then you and your spouse are on even playing fields, making incremental steps towards good habits that you would like to institute.

- **Call out your family members when they make excuses.** It is bound to happen. I've been known to do the same thing. When it really comes down to it, our worlds are small. We are concerned about tasks that directly affect ourselves and we think we know everything at times. So, you might be faced with a situation where your son makes up excuses as to why he didn't perform an important task, like get the trash to the curb before the garbage truck arrived or take your rent check to the landlord's office before 5:00 pm when the office closed. He might try to bring up schoolwork or an unexpected phone call. This is when you need to gently ask your excuse-making family member, "Are you being honest with yourself?" Don't ask family members if they are being honest with you; that is irrelevant and will just escalate your issue. Believe me, I have seen teenage children double down on excuses and fight with angry tears in defending tenuous positions. You don't want to go down that road. Instead, take a deep breath and just ask them if they are being honest with themselves. After all, things happen, and we have not perfected time travel yet. (If we did, I'd have already gone back in time and bought a bunch of tech stocks, reaped my rewards, and purchased several beach houses.) You are not going to be able to go back and re-do the task. Right now, you need to fix the problem and impress upon your wayward child the fact that some tasks need to be done no matter what and that excuses are not part of the solution. Instead, enlist him or her in brainstorming ways to fix the issue. Bonus! You have just added problem solving to their repertoire of life skills.

This last strategy is the most difficult one to keep in place in your chaotic household. You can get people to do small scale projects, like clean a wardrobe, organize a kitchen drawer, or even spend a weekend overhauling the garage. However, it is more challenging to get your people to make a mind shift and culture change. This is an area where you are going to need to employ all your patience and positivity. There will be setbacks. We all fall off the wagon on fixing our vices and this area is no exception. When that happens, simply try one of the other approaches, like enlisting help, talking to your family about items that spark joy or tackling one area of the home that needs immediate organization. You can get back to change later— once your family members get another organizational win under their belts and are ready to try implementing order into their daily routines so that things do not get so out of hand.

CHAPTER 7 CHEAT SHEET

To sum up, here are some strategies to approach the cluttered spaces in your home:

1. **The Do I Still Like It? Approach or "Spark Joy" Approach**

   Ask your family members what items they particularly like and enjoy. Organize and keep these items. Get rid of objects that are not adding value or happiness to the family. Definitely get rid of items that are actually a burden to the household.

2. **The Valuable Real Estate Approach**

   Assess the important or high value places in your home. Make sure those areas only contain the best stuff. Ensure that these areas stay decluttered and not over-full.

3. **The Pareto Principle or the 80/20 Rule**

   Assess areas of the home and keep the 20 percent of items that are regularly used, worn, or viewed. Then review the 80 percent that just take up space and are rarely used. Can you pack up or remove some of these items to make your space less cluttered and more accessible?

4. **The Creation of a Personal Oasis Approach**

   Let everyone plan out a personal haven or spot in the home. Allow each person to have full domain over that one area. Ensure that other family members respect the personal oasis of others and do not bring in their own stuff.

5   **The Hand Holding or Companionship Approach**

Figure out which family members prefer to work alone, and which members need companionship and support. Find people to help the family members that need extra help.

6   **The Tackle the Scary First Approach**

Consider a large-scale project for your family members if they like challenges and prefer a big pay-off. Use this win to encourage people to seek smaller victories in organizing the home.

7   **The First Responder Approach**

Send in the first responder to assess the area and do some preliminary help in getting the project started. Have this person or team come in and pull everything out in one place for your ADHD people to see everything at once and make decisions.

8   **The Embrace the Clutter Approach**

Spend a little time with your collectors and help them create a vision of a carefully curated collection that does NOT take over your home but that is visually appealing and contained. If there is just too much stuff for the home, investigate some external storage options to keep the items off-property.

9   **The Little and Often Approach**

Encourage everyone to work on incremental steps to keep the house more orderly over time. Break down big tasks into small steps for your ADHD people. Try to take time to reinforce successful behavior and reward small steps that become daily habits.

(8)

HELPING YOUR FAMILY CREATE AND MAINTAIN THEIR OWN SCHEDULES

Now that you have gotten your home in some better order and worked together to create some nice spaces, it is a good time to help your chaotic family institute some order into their daily schedule of living. **It is time to go big or go home!** Again—your free spirits might just float and fritter and make living look so colorful and fun. But in my family, we have no trust funds to finance our lives, so we all must find a way to get educated or trained and find a job to support ourselves.

As parents, our hope for our children is that they will forge ahead and live a happy life. Some people sit back and hope that happiness will just land in their laps, but in my experience, happiness comes from planning and achievement. As Arnold Palmer said about his golf game, "It's a funny thing, the more I practice the luckier I get." Practicing means putting forth some effort which will result in meeting goals. Helping your family members come up with some simple, easy to implement daily strategies will give them some framework for life. As an organized person yourself, you probably already have a system that works for you. In the next several pages, I will discuss some systems that you might consider for your chaotic family members who do not want to simply adopt your system. These are in no particular order. Read through the different techniques and discuss with your crew what systems might work for them. Then try out the different ideas. You will find out through trial and error what methods stick with different members of your household.

Maintain Multiple Calendars

This one seemed crazy to me at first, but I have come to embrace it myself. Back in the day I kept a paper calendar, but as technology boomed, I transitioned to using my smartphone calendar and a To-do application for all my scheduling needs. After all, business associates were always sending out Google calendar reminders and making me accept digital invitations, so I just learned and adapted to putting everything on a machine. My husband and I shared a "cloud" so our calendars synced, and we could see each other's schedules. This cut down on couples' arguments by half. There were no remonstrations like, "I didn't know where you were!" or "You didn't tell me the kids had soccer practice!" If I didn't answer my phone, Todd could simply look at the calendar and see that I was holding a staff meeting or at the dentist.

I truly thought this worked great for me and assumed that my Millennial and Gen Z kids would embrace technology and utilize their smartphones for all calendar activities. I would help my kids to put alerts on their phones and wonder why they were still late for practice or missed important events.

Basically, I did not account for the fact that my children could not see the big picture. **Vision is important for everyone.** This is why we went through the practice of developing a family mission and vision board for creating order. Thus, it only makes sense that our family members might need to see a daily, weekly, or monthly vision to get organized and tackle jobs and projects.

Therefore, my family members have created a multiple calendar system whereby we keep a paper calendar AND utilize our smart phones. The great thing about the paper calendar is that you can see a monthly view as well as individual appointments on separate daily pages. Seeing the monthly view lets you anticipate upcoming appointments that might need some preparation or advance planning concerning rides, travel, or babysitting. I know for a fact that I am more productive now that I keep a monthly calendar on my kitchen island to view while I am making tea or letting the dog outside. That monthly view is my "look ahead and see what is coming" reminder, or as I like to say it — *Game of Thrones* style, "Winter is coming." I always like walking into the kitchen and seeing one of the kids thumbing through the paper calendar. No matter what level of disorder they live in, your family is genuinely curious about upcoming family events. Use this curiosity to your benefit and help your kids see the big vision. The monthly views let you see and anticipate.

Smartphones, then, are the workhorses that create immediate alerts and reminders. They are the short-term memory devices that get us through the day. If I have an event that is out of the ordinary, I make sure I put on a 15-minute reminder AHEAD of the time I need to leave, ensuring that I don't get wrapped up in work or forget an important meeting. If you are a daydreamer or on that ADHD spectrum, you might consider placing a couple alerts, just to make sure you stay on track for your most important events and appointments.

Wendy Keenan Myers

Create and Maintain ONE Family Calendar

When the kids were home and in school, I also utilized a family calendar printed out on paper and kept in the kitchen. You might also consider the use of a chalkboard wall or whiteboard where all the important tasks and appointments for the week are written out for everyone to see and visualize. After all, if you all live together and rely on each other for transportation and reminders, you need to share your information.

Now you might be saying, "Why can't I just leave out my personal paper calendar for all to see?" That is, for sure, a valid point, and you are welcome to go forth and share your calendar. I do this now that my husband and I are empty nesters, and we just have to be accountable to each other. However, when the kids were all home and things were more chaotic, it was better for me to make a separate family calendar that only listed the kids' activities and our family vacations and events. Having all my minutia about work meetings, charitable events, health appointments and my elaborate to-do list was something the kids just did not need in their lives. It was better to let the focus simply be on the tasks that related to them. This kept the kids from being bogged down with all those tasks and allowed them to learn how to keep a calendar and develop their own skills and confidence in scheduling — not to mention the fact that I didn't need three girls to know about every time I went to get a massage or pedicure and listen to them try to make the case that they needed those services (not until you have a job and your own money, kids!).

Another great aspect of the family calendar is that EVERYONE can participate and add their important events and information. Kids can come home from school and write in things like "pajama day at school" for next Tuesday or they can leave permission slips right there for you to review and sign. Your significant other can make a notation that she needs paperclips and oven cleaner on the calendar entry for the weekly shopping day or your Amazon needs list. If you all get into the habit of looking at the calendar, you can even leave notes for each other, ideas that you want to share with everyone or reminders of tasks like walking the dog or checking the mailbox.

Develop Personalized Reminder Systems

My kids would often accuse me of treating each child differently, and they were right. Each child is different, so each child needs a different reminder and scheduling system. Some kids need to hear a rundown of all the events for the day, so they are prepared and ready for the events ahead. Other kids want to hear the bare minimum and just approach the day with a more carefree attitude. Hearing about everything that must be accomplished in advance might be too stressful for some of your family members. Instead of getting an itemized listing of all the errands you are doing, like: post office, bank, get a key made, head to the mall, get some dinner, then stop at the store for milk, bread and fruit and then go home to pack lunches for the next day—your family might rather hear a boiled down version of the day—like: we are headed to the mall and to dinner. Then, as the day enfolds, you can simply insert in the other tasks that need to be accomplished.

When our youngest daughter was receiving cancer treatments, she didn't want to know the minutia of what needed done, like pill regime, daily infusions, appointment times, etc. She only wanted to know the overall vision and the ending date. She didn't care about the science behind the treatments or any other medical mumbo-jumbo (her words, not mine!). Since she had a dedicated support system of her family, we could take on those issues for her and simply allow Isabelle to focus on a healthy, positive outcome and to dream of the day, nine months later, when she would be free from the treatment regime. But, of course, she could not ignore scheduling all together. I made the calendar and the pill system, but she had to check off the days and take her pills. She had to drive herself to treatments and figure out ways to do homework while plugged into machines. But to really get through the arduous process, she needed to leave out some unessential details, like medical theory and such, and focus on the prize. You will have people like this in your family that don't enjoy the nitty gritty details and will need to see a big vision to understand why those details are important in achieving that dream. Keep this factor in mind when trying out different techniques.

Some of your kids might like a personal whiteboard system where they write down important events in their bedroom or in a prominent place like the bathroom mirror. Others might work better with colorful sticky notes attached to the mirror, walls, or bedside stand. And others might just want to use a paper calendar or planner notebook.

There is a proliferation of ADHD and organizational apps for smart phones that might help your family members as well. Of course, these phone apps are only as good as the information and effort that you put into the program. But having a program with prompts to put in tasks and projects can help your organizationally challenged ones tremendously. Some apps will track how long you work on the computer or alert you when you seem to be distracted or off track. Some apps also assist with the estimation of task time which is particularly good for people who chronically under or overestimate the time for project completion. Within your family, you might even consider an app that allows you to all link in a team, which can be helpful for those individuals who need to be accountable to someone else to start and complete tasks. Some apps that have been noteworthy for ADHD assistance include: RescueTime, Asana, todoist, OFFTIME, Evernote, getinflow, Headspace, Focus@Will and Pomodor.

Anna-Claire, my most organized daughter and a 10th grade English teacher, recently disclosed her morning routine to me. She sets 7 morning alarms on her iPhone. Yes, you read that right, SEVEN alarms.

She prefers to be overprepared, and she likes the feeling of knowing that she has a few more minutes to lounge in bed before she must get up and start the day. And she likes to push that snooze button several times! My daughter also has a long wind down time routine that she uses at night to decompress. She likes to get into her pajamas and go to bed around 9:00 pm. Then for the next hour or so, she reads her book or listens to a podcast. Lastly, she turns on some gentle white noise and uses that background to slowly drift off to sleep. While I find her routine to sleep and wake up to be overly orchestrated, this is what works for Anna-Claire. Some people in your family might need those buffer times in the day that help them de-stress, unwind and recharge for the tasks that lie ahead.

It is important, then, to not just schedule duties and chores, but to also plan out time for self-care. There has been some chatter recently about "revenge bedtime procrastination" on social media sites. Basically, this is where an adult chooses NOT to go to sleep because he or she values the freedom of late-night hours over the need for sleep. This often affects people who are overwhelmed in their daily routines—who exercise this "revenge" over the possibility of sleep as a way to regain control in their lives. Busy parents, caregivers and employees spend their days meeting the needs of others and never getting moments of time to themselves to decompress or do something enjoyable. So, all those things that they wanted to do all day—like read a book, scroll social media, watch videos, craft, or play video games—now take the place of much-needed sleep. In her 2023 article for Verywellmind.com, Kendra Cherry notes that the concept of bedtime procrastination first showed up in a 2014 scientific paper in *Frontiers in Psychology*. She further describes how revenge bedtime procrastination often starts small, with people knowing that they should get to sleep but still choosing to online shop, scroll through social media and do other things that keep them awake. Of course, the lack of sleep results in all sorts of negative consequences from health issues to decreased daytime productivity. When tackling the daily routine, therefore, it is important to plan out things like alone time, hobby time, social media time and bedtime.

Also as part of a daily routine, everyone needs some sort of to-do list and there are several ways to create these lists. The main concept is to write things down as you think about the task that needs to be completed. You can use your smartphone, a calendar planner, a notebook, an index card, or the back of an envelope. The main thing is to have things written down, so you don't waste brain power trying to remember things and you don't stress out over the sheer number of things that need to be done. One technique that works for some people is to take some time at work on Friday afternoon to write down everything that needs to be started on Monday. That way you don't spend your weekend stressed out and trying to remember everything that you need to do for the next week. Alternatively, you can take a couple of moments on Sunday night to look at your calendar and think about the next day. This is a good time to chunk out to-do items into a few bullet points so that you can hit the ground running on Monday morning with a clear plan of what needs to be accomplished for the week.

Believe it or not, your ADHD members of the family might need to write down tasks that you would consider obvious. For example, I have two daughters that got so focused on studying or doing projects at school that they would forget to eat. Their stress manifested as single-minded behavior that meant they would forget about self-care. I would ask them to set reminders on their phones to take breaks and eat snacks. I even mailed them both snack boxes and nutrient-rich drinks to their dorms so they would have easy things on hand to intake during these stressful times.

We affectionately call my husband the absent-minded professor because he is often oblivious to things of this world while he is contemplating more creative and deeper thoughts. However, this means that he often forgets to take his blood pressure medications and do tasks that we discussed. I will ask him to forward me an important email and it will take several prompts to get the task completed. For him, a detailed to-do list is imperative. He needs to check off the tasks and write down more basic things like exercise and take medications or he will simply forget that they were important items on his daily agenda. This goes back to the need to schedule items that contribute to your overall health.

Many experts say that you should just prioritize and write down three manageable goals for the day and if productivity allows, you can move onto some other, less important tasks. However, ADHD folks need more guidance and orientation to stay on task, thus requiring a more extensive list. If you have someone off-the-charts ADHD in your household, you might sit with him or her and establish a daily routine list to help get started. And put down every detail of the day, starting with getting out of bed and listing out each daily task. While it might seem ridiculous to you, people with ADHD forget that they need to brush their hair when they get sidetracked by some other idea that comes into their minds. This running, personalized list might be the impetus they need to get started on a more productive and less stressful daily routine.

Furthermore, people with ADHD often have difficulty with task shifting. In research studies, scientists have found that despite the urban myth of multitasking, people can only focus on ONE thing at a time. In fact, when we are interrupted on important tasks with an alarm from an incoming text or a phone call, we lose, on average, 17 minutes in shifting our attention back to our original tasks. A good technique to keep focused and not derailed with distractions is to jot down reminders as things happen. For example, in the middle of studying, my daughter might remember that she needs to change laundry or pick up her mail. Instead of stopping in the middle of an important task to do these things, she simply writes those things on a whiteboard so she can finish the studying. Later she will check her board and see what other things need done. If you know that you are easily distracted, tell your loved ones NOT to ask you to drop everything to help them find something or to do a menial task that can wait until later. Instead, jot that task down on your running to-do list or ask them to prompt you later when you have finished your more important work.

To stay on task, your ADHD family members may need to learn to protect their focus in other ways. Talk to them about turning off ringtones and alarms on technological devices. For your people who want noise in the background, help them find white noise or soothing background music to take the place of television shows and TikTok videos. If you are someone like me that has the compulsion to keep checking the phone for emails and text messages so you don't miss anything important, learn to give everyone an emergency phone number that you will answer and carve out bigger blocks of technology-free time to think, create and stay focused. Staying on our smartphones all the time is just another bad habit that many of us have cultivated, but one that we can also unlearn. Train yourself to pay attention to others at work and at home. Fight the impulse to pull out your phone and scroll through messages when other people are talking to you. Once you start distancing yourself from the distractions, you can control these fun diversions in smaller blocks of time or as rewards AFTER doing focused work for several hours.

Some people may need reminders right in front of their faces. For example, my mother-in-law has utilized a reminder system with her husband for decades. My father-in-law loves to run errands and volunteers to do most of the shopping, dropping off and picking up tasks; however, he is easily distracted and needs help with staying on schedule. My mother-in-law writes him out a to-do list on a 3.5" index card that he can then stick in the pocket of his shirt. While he runs errands and goes around town, he can easily pull out the card to see what he needs to do next.

Post-it notes are also great ways to snag the attention of your co-workers. My teacher daughter has fifty different students asking her to check grades or resend emails. Since it is difficult to remember everything that people ask verbally, Anna-Claire asks her students to write reminders for her on post-it notes that they can attach to her laptop where she will see them. For your family, find out where the best place is to leave notes that will help them remember important tasks—like near car keys, by the coffee pot or posted to the bathroom mirror.

My oldest daughter, Maddie, also uses notes instead of emailing people at her laboratory. She is a pathology resident and regularly must ask her superiors to look at reports or call patients. Instead of emailing her superiors and running the risk of the messages being buried in the in-box, she posts bright colored post-it notes to their desks or laptops with a handwritten request along with a friendly smiley face. Her bosses are seated at their desk when they see her notes, so they are probably in a better position to look at a report or make the necessary phone call. When Maddie really wants to get her attending physician's attention, she uses her special sloth post-it notes. Like she says, "How can you ignore a cute little sloth post-it?" Since she is often in the role of the middleman, Maddie has found a way to get peoples' attention and manage the chaos of her workplace. Half of all organization is just communicating well with others and Maddie's post-it notes are a great way for her to direct her thoughts and communicate with people.

Creating imaginary deadlines might also be a helpful strategy for your chronic procrastinators. If you live with a procrastinator or someone with ADHD, you have been there before: your disorganized child waits until the last minute to do a larger project and then everyone in the household is pulled into the crisis zone. You can, instead, help them create earlier imaginary deadlines that will help your children to get and to stay on task. And you can tie those deadlines to rewards. If the goals are met, the child can use the car that weekend or go to the movies with their friends. I also sometimes tell some of my family members an earlier departure time so that I know that we will all be ready and on time for our event. (Family: If you are reading this, you know who you are!) Of course, I try to use this technique sparingly, for only really important events, because I don't want to enable their procrastination habit. Instead, I prefer to create a prompting system that empowers the procrastinators to take control of their schedules and learn the better habit of leaving on time and respecting others' time schedules.

ne thing that will always be hard for your ADHD folks is remembering and keeping appointments. My youngest daughter once missed a hair appointment that she was really looking forward to and was reduced to tears. This was a much-anticipated, fun appointment and she missed it—even with several alerts placed on her smartphone. Often, people with ADHD get working on a project or daydreaming about grandiose plans and lose all track of time. Alerts can help, but sometimes you need a back-up plan—especially for very important appointments. In our household, we have come up with an appointment-buddy system. Isabelle and Todd (our chronic appointment missers) let others know about their events and ask these buddies to be their final reminders. Here is how this works: Isabelle makes an appointment and asks her buddy to put that event on his or her calendar. Then, ON that day, if Isabelle remembers the appointment and is on her way there, she will text her buddy. If the buddy does not get a text, he or she calls Isabelle to prompt her to stop daydreaming and get to that appointment.

As you can see, there are all sorts of reminder systems. Sometimes I think that we get caught up in what is the "right way." But here's the thing—there is no ONE right way. It's okay to elicit help and it's okay to work together. Try different strategies to see what works in your household.

Create Specific Prompts

Prompts can be a great way for individuals to implement daily reminders and create new habits. For example, you might pop in some chewing gum as a reminder to go for a walk or sit at your computer and work on a research project. Some people like wearing a hair band or rubber band around their wrists that they can tug on or snap every time they feel like eating, smoking, drinking or some other bad habit that they are trying to break. Basically, you choose a behavioral, visual, or vocal prompt that reminds you of the task you need to do or to avoid.

You are probably aware of the "Hang in There" motivational cat poster that may have hung in your high school or at a physician's office. And every day as you scroll through social media, you probably come across motivational memes and gifs posted by friends and family. Obviously, we are drawn to positive sayings and visuals as tools to stop and focus ourselves on something good in our lives. You can use this positive visual prompt to focus yourself. For example, if you are working on a thesis, post a positive quotation in front of your computer that your eyes will see when you space out from your laptop. Or post a motivational poster in front of your elliptical machine or workout area to keep you on task to complete a morning workout.

My daughter Isabelle prefers visual prompts. If objects are not readily available to her, she will not see them. She recently created a prompting area for herself by the front door to her apartment. She simply placed a hot pink cubby by the door and as she comes in from work or school, she dumps out her pockets, purse and backpack into the cubby. Since she often changes totes bags, purses, and coats, she was losing her college ID, keys and important papers. Now, everything is in one place, and she has the prompt she needs to gather up important objects before she leaves home for the day.

My husband's visual prompt from me is to gather important papers or items for his errand list, like return a tool to Lowes or drop off a plant to his sister, and to put these items underneath his car keys or right in the path of the doorway so he trips over them on his way out. You might create a key bowl or area by your front door where you put important school papers, store returns, bank deposits and other items that need completed the next day. Establishing a visual prompt habit, like putting your keys in the same place every evening when you return home, means you are less likely to lose that item and waste precious time the next time you need to go somewhere.

For my sister-in-law, Jamie, a major prompt for her every day is to simply put on her shoes. She runs a busy household and manages a family business. However, she is easily distracted. For example, her phone might ding with a message and before she knows it, Jamie has spent thirty minutes reading an email that could have waited until later in the day, or worse, scrolling through social media. That half hour will put her whole day behind because then the mail carrier might drop off the mail, her husband might call with a question or the dogs will want outside, putting her further behind with distractions. By putting on her shoes, Jamie prompts herself to realize that she needs to leave the house to do her daily walk or head to work. It makes it less likely that she will traipse back through the house or flop down on her couch. For her, the shoes signal her brain for action. Other people do this with workouts. The prompt is to put on athletic clothing to, in turn, prompt you to add a workout, run or walk to your day.

My father-in-law does a lot of shopping for the family business. His prompt is to carry a brightly colored zippered bank bag in his truck. As he shops for tools and supplies, he places every receipt into the bank bag. Until he had this item to prompt him, he would stuff receipts in the truck, in his pockets, in random Ziploc bags, etc. It became problematic for him to find things and to match expenses on the credit card accounts and bank statements. Think about areas where your family could use a prompt to help them take care of an important task.

My twin nieces play a lot of volleyball, and their mom has come up with a visual and tactile prompt to help them stay better organized. The volleyball gear bags are kept in the same place on their back porch. Before getting in the car, the girls must physically touch everything in the bag and check off the items on a cheat sheet that they have written up for the bag. Since most of the gear is black, it is easy to miss seeing knee pads or socks in the huge bag along with all the other stuff like shoes, water bottles, snacks, and uniforms. The touch test means that the twins have verified that everything is there, not just viewed something that looked like knee pads or socks and assumed that everything was present.

In addition to visual and behavioral prompts, you might consider a vocal mantra to help yourself cue the desired behavior. For example, when you are carrying around some item of trash in your house, create a vocal prompt in your head (or even say it aloud to yourself!), like "Don't put this down, put it in trash." If you need to remind yourself of an important daily goal, repeat it over and over in your head, so that you are not sidetracked by other, less important items.

You can suggest visual, behavioral, and vocal prompts to your ADHD and otherwise organizationally challenged family members as tools to improve focus and steer attention. Focusing on positive associations will help your family members feel better about needing these mantras and visual cues to get and stay on task.

Consider Utilizing the Pomodoro Technique

The Pomodoro Technique was created in the late 1980s by Francesco Cirillo as a proactive way to tackle his tendency to procrastinate while attending college. Basically, this is a time management technique where you complete a 25-minute segment of focused work then stop and take a five-minute break. After four consecutive work segments, you take a longer break of 15 to 30 minutes. Cirillo named the technique for the Italian word for tomato, "pomodoro," because he used a tomato-shaped kitchen timer when experimenting with different time intervals for his study sessions. Thus, each work segment of 25 minutes is called a "pomodoro." Based on Cirillo's research, 25 minutes is the optimum amount of time to do quality work before the worker becomes tired, bored, or unfocused. Also, by setting a timer and buckling down to do work, you minimize the propensity to procrastinate or to try to multitask. Since your time segments are small and manageable, following this system can keep your organizationally challenged people from becoming too anxious about tasks and can foster productivity.

The key here is FOCUS. You need to drown out the background and minimize the interruptions. Thus, you don't check your phone for texts and social media updates, and you silence the beeps on electronic notifications. You might have music or white noise if that helps with focus but avoid television and other background noise that will distract you from the task at hand. For some of your family members, finding that focus point might be a real challenge. Come up with a plan together, even if that means you need to take their cell phone for 25 minutes, you put them in a quiet, secluded part of the home or you park them at the local library.

Once focus has been established, figure out breaks that contrast with the task at hand. For example, if you are sitting at a computer working away for 25 minutes, your break might be to walk to the mailbox or do some yoga stretches. If you are cleaning and organizing stuff, your break might be to sit down and eat a snack or scroll through social media on your phone. Make sure that your pomodoro worker takes the breaks at the end of the working segment. If you keep on trucking away after the 25 minutes of focus, you run the risk of losing interest and focus and stopping without ever going back to that task. This is unfortunate if this is your child who is cleaning his or her closet and decides to just walk away, leaving a huge mess. Or if your husband doesn't finish a bill paying session and you end up with big late fees that could have been avoided. And adding in those timed breaks allows your people to de-stress and build some enjoyment into the busy day which is important for getting back to tasks and to keep from devolving into revenge bedtime procrastination and other destructive habits.

Do the Hardest Task First

Like the "tackle the scary first" method of household organization, this technique makes you do your hardest or most disliked task of the day, first thing in the morning. In his book, *Eat That Frog!*, time management expert Brian Tracy uses the metaphor of eating a live frog to demonstrate the importance of getting the worst task done and out of the way. He postulates that if you must eat a real ugly frog in the morning—that is the worst thing that will happen to you all day, so you might as well go forth and get that out of the way!

However, the procrastinators in your life will try to do anything they can to avoid eating the frog. They will try to defer the task or choose several unimportant tasks to do instead. Their fear will keep them from even starting to eat the frog, and by burying their head in the sand or going on to other, meaningless tasks, the procrastinators hope that the frog will simply hop away. But you and I know this will not happen. The hard task will still be there, and the longer that it goes undone, the more difficult and scarier it will start to loom in our minds.

In his research on procrastinators, Dr. Joseph Ferrari, cites the importance of reward systems. His procrastination research showed that normal time management tools were ineffective in overcoming chronic procrastination. Instead, his research showed that it was more effective to tie unpleasant tasks to more rewarding ones, just to get the task accomplished. For example, if you hate exercise but have the goal of using a treadmill three times a week, tie that task to something enjoyable, like watching a favorite show on Netflix or reading a juicy romance novel. If you have a difficult phone call to make, do it right after you get ready in the morning and before you lose your nerve. After the telephone call is completed, reward yourself with your morning coffee or 30 minutes of social media scrolling—or whatever you find relaxing after a stressful situation.

In fact, the research supports that reward systems work for all types of organization and completion of tasks. Often, we want to cite the consequences or bad things that happen if tasks do not get done. However, remember that you are dealing with folks who chronically procrastinate and lack focus. They often decide to NOT take action and choose less stressful activities like gaming or watching television over tackling a complicated or difficult task. Negative consequences can become routine for procrastinators. They always have late fees on bills, they are always passed up for promotion at work, and they always lose points on homework assignments that are turned in after the deadline. You can't hit them with more bad consequences. Instead, focus on something positive that your procrastinator can collect as a reward. Decluttering might result in a beautiful, stress-free haven for him or her in the home. Sitting down and doing the college application will result in the opportunity to attend college in the fall. Going to the post office early to pay taxes will result in more money since no late fees will be applied. Accentuate the positive to gain more buy in from the people who need that extra motivation to take on important tasks.

Often your hardest task is the most important task. It is the one that will help you propel your job forward or repair a relationship. For example, you want a pay raise but are afraid of confrontation. You will not get that raise until you go to your employer with a compelling case for why you deserve that raise. Your boss is not going to spontaneously reward you and might need that prompt to provide that benefit. After all, you don't always get what you deserve in life—but you will get what you are able to negotiate. It is uncomfortable and scary, but it is the roadblock you need to face to get to that next level and reach your goal of better pay benefits.

Really, this method is just inviting your people to start already and take action. In her popular TED talk and her published book, *The Five Second Rule: Transform Your Life, Work, and Confidence with Everyday Courage,* Mel Robbins discusses how this approach helped her transform her life when she was in a cycle of depression and joblessness. She discusses the importance of acting before your brain has the opportunity to shut down the idea or follow a path of distraction. So as soon as the idea hits, you simply count down: 5-4-3-2-1 and then start the task. I often employ this simple approach when my morning alarm goes off for my workout class. If it is cold or rainy, I am tempted to hit snooze and skip the class, but then I remember that pesky five second rule and I count down in my head, making sure my feet are hitting the ground when I hit the one mark.

Sometimes your frog is a really big task that is just too daunting to face. In fact, you might not even know where to start. And the ADHD members of your family lack focus to even start to take on these huge frogs. This is where the next method can come in handy to help them find a way to make the big task appear as a list of smaller, more manageable items.

Break Tasks Down into a Step-by-Step Process

Many experts suggest the chunk method as a way to achieve bigger goals. For this technique, you list out your process in baby steps that you can follow and check off on the journey to meet your goal. This is where you take each goal and make separate lists with step-by-step instructions or bullet points to follow. This is especially helpful for large-scale or grandiose tasks that you might find overwhelming, like spring cleaning or winterizing your property. Obviously, all the tasks can't be accomplished in a single time period, so you chunk out the items so that you can plug away at the tasks, step by step and over time.

A noteworthy proponent of this technique is David Allen, a productivity expert and author of *Getting Things Done: The Art of Stress-free Productivity*. In his book, he introduces his productivity method:

GTD (getting things done) where you simply remove the myriad of pesky tasks and burdens from your mind by writing them down and further breaking down the tasks into actionable work items with time limits. According to Allen, the entire system reduces stress because your mind will not get distracted with unknowns when everything is written down. Since stress comes with uncertainty, Allen emphasizes the importance of closing what he calls "open loops" or "incompletes" by writing down the next step in the process of completing each task. That way you are not focused on issues where you have no easy resolution and don't know the next part of the process to achieve completion. The next day is easier because you now have a clear idea of what to do next.

Artificial intelligence has made this a much easier process. Check out the website **https://goblin.tools/About** created by Bram De Buyser, a freelance software engineer. At the time of this publication, website usage is free, but you can purchase an app on your smartphone for a nominal fee if you prefer. In the application, you type in a task you want to achieve like "make homemade macaroni and cheese" or "write a book." Then you click on the button and—using artificial intelligence—that task is then split out into individual tasks which can each be clicked on to develop further. In fact, De Buyser's tagline for the website is "Breaking things down so you don't." He further advertises it as a tool to help "neurodivergent people with tasks they find overwhelming or difficult." There are separate buttons for creating to do lists, for finding recipes using ingredients you have in your kitchen, for helping to judge the tone of your text messages, for organizing all the mixed-up information in your brain, for formalizing or downgrading your writing for readability and for estimating the time that it will take for you to perform a task. Honestly when you use the website or application, you will feel like you live at Hogwarts and are using magic to enhance your life.

Eliminate Busy Work from Your Daily Routine

In his book, *Automate Your Busywork: Do Less, Achieve More, and Save Your Brain for the Big Stuff*, author Aytekin Tank (CEO of Jotform) discusses the proliferation of busy work and how it impacts our productivity and creativity. Tank postulates that people are bad at estimating the time it will take to complete tasks. In fact, he cites statistics from the *Huffington Post* that demonstrate that only 17 percent of the population can accurately estimate the time it takes to finish a job. Since we are bad at analyzing timed tasks, we need to try to get rid of unnecessary tasks to allow for the extra time we might need to finish important jobs.

Remember the Pareto principle from the last chapter? In general, 20 percent of our effort creates 80 percent of our results. Thus, we need to figure out the most important 20 percent and concentrate our efforts there. The remaining 80 percent of daily and weekly tasks are probably a lot of busy work activities that could be decreased or eliminated.

Busy work includes all the little tasks that never end, like laundry, checking email, getting groceries, etc. Tank suggests that everyone perform an audit of their busy work. For example, time yourself on how long you spend going through emails, folding laundry, running to the store and so on. This audit will, no doubt, be eye opening. For me, it was shocking how much time I spent going to several different stores for grocery shopping. And I found that my biggest time waster was Walmart. If I wasn't efficient and prepared with a good list, I wasted a lot of time going back and forth from the front to the far end of the store, often getting waylaid along the way with looking at end cap displays and seeing people I know. For me, ordering groceries online and scheduling a pickup became a huge time saver. While it was sometimes fun to roam around the store, this time-consuming shopping was really keeping me from more important tasks like running my business, writing this book, or exercising. The busy work, in essence, became my procrastination tool. I put that task in front of the more important ones because it was easier, sometimes fun, and quickly checked off from a to-do list.

In running my real estate business, I found that I was doing all sorts of busy work that needed to be delegated to others or eliminated. For example, I loved putting in rents to the system and going to the bank. However, it was more important for my staff to do this task. First, they knew the tenants and rents inside out and had way more knowledge than me. They knew things like the fact that an agency paid half the rent, or the roommate was paying late this month and had a payment plan in place. Second, putting in rents to the system was sometimes time-consuming and was keeping me from important things like analyzing my income and expenses and comparing these amounts with previous periods. Since we accept no cash and we utilize a rental property software program, my employees have all the tools to do this job well and without risk of missing or losing payments. I can simply audit deposits periodically and reconcile accounts each month, two tasks that are much less time-consuming. Surely you have tasks like this in your household or job as well—tasks that you like to do but really should pass on to someone else so that you can finish other things.

It is easy to outsource things you hate to do, which for me is lawncare and clean bathrooms. But sometimes you enjoy tasks or like checking them off your list so you can feel productive. That is fine if you have the time and are accomplishing all your other goals. However, if you haven't finished that important project at work, finished the baby quilt you are making for a friend or completed your personal goal of becoming a real estate agent, then you are putting things in front of you that are distracting you from more important work and you need to get a handle on that busy work.

Furthermore, some tasks do not even need to be finished. I know that is crazy talk to some of you, but bear with me. Do you generate reports at work that no one ever reads? Do you attend meetings that add no value to your life or the lives of others? Do you focus energy on things that just are not important to you or your family? Recently, I had an epiphany when decorating the house for Christmas. Every year we acquired a real tree for the family room and put up a pre-lit tree in the formal rooms of the house. Since we live in an older home, we rarely venture into the front, formal rooms of the home, preferring to stay in the cozy family room that is connected to the kitchen. The formal tree was seen by no one, unless we had a big party that used the whole downstairs. Since my kids were all at college or on their own, I eliminated the real tree; it was too much work and created a mess! I moved the pre-lit tree to the family room and pared down the rest of the decorations. No one complained. The house was still festive and decorated nicely. For many years, I was over-decorating. After the holidays, I took the opportunity to pare down all the decorations to make more room in the basement. The entire elimination was a win-win scenario.

My daughter, Anna-Claire, recently told me about an issue she regularly faces at work which is a huge busy work issue. When colleagues tried to plan a meeting, they sent out a massive email or text thread asking for everyone's input in developing the meeting time. Then everyone answers with things like, "I can do it anytime," "Any day but Wednesday," or "I'm only free on Mondays and Wednesdays between 9:00 am and 11:00 am." It then takes someone a lot of time to compile the answers and go back and forth on the email or text thread to get the meeting scheduled. Also, this wastes everyone's time on the thread who is distracted with all the options and the going back-and-forth discussion. Anna-Claire's contention was that the meeting should be scheduled up front by the organizer who can then move it if people have difficult conflicts. Giving people too many options can be a huge time waster. If you allow too much input, you will drive yourself crazy trying to accommodate everyone and find the perfect time. However, if you set the date and time and put out the meeting invite, colleagues might be able to move things on their own to make the appointed meeting.

Other tasks can be automated or adjusted so they can be finished in a more orderly, efficient fashion. Artificial intelligence (AI) is an obvious example for automation. As you type a text on your smart phone, the phone itself tries to finish your thought. (For the record, I am old school, and ZERO artificial intelligence was used in the writing of this book!) If you have ever used the chat feature when talking with an airline, online store, or utility company, then you have seen firsthand how these companies are able to automate routine tasks to free up personnel to work on more complex tasks and to save on staffing overall. I utilize AI when creating content for my business social media sites so that I don't have to spend hours creating and posting every day. According to a 2017 report by the McKinsey Global Institute, a third of the jobs worldwide will be obsolete by the year 2030, simply because of the proliferation of artificial intelligence. As technology continues to improve, your productivity and success will suffer if you don't keep up with the trends in how to automate tasks.

Most of us hate change and we continue doing things the same way over and over just because these tasks have always been done that way. For example, I had a job of doing medical billing and dictation for an assisted living home. To help the providers, I kept my lists in room order number for all the residents. However, the residents often switched rooms and people got moved around and I was forever updating that list. To bill the insurance companies, I kept a log that was in alphabetical order for myself. So, when I got the medical notes on the roster from the provider, I had to shuffle back and forth among several sheets of paper to enter in my data. I kept this system for years; I mean 20 plus years! Just recently, billing insurance carriers became more onerous as patients chose all different Medicare options, and the work was taking me over four hours longer each week. After thinking about how I could improve things, I took a couple hours of time to revamp my system, to make all the roster, dictation, and insurance intake systems flow in alphabetical order to make my job easier. The providers had no problem because they simply worked through the list at the desk with nursing staff after going from room to room. I can only imagine how many hours I could have saved over the years if I had made this change earlier! Take the time now to analyze your work and set up clear systems, and you will not make my mistake.

Take time with your family to review your household tasks. Figure out items that are urgent and need done immediately, like fixing your car so you can get to work or attending an important doctor's appointment. Next, figure out tasks that are important to the overall health and wellbeing of the family, like making nutritious meals, exercising, and having family bonding time. Then figure out tasks that can be delegated to others or eliminated all together because they just do not add value. Once you all start communicating important needs, you will figure out what items are just no longer necessary and what items need to be prioritized for completion.

And while you are at it, think about volunteer tasks that are keeping you from meeting your other goals in life that you have been doing for a while now but that need to be passed on to someone else. Don't get me wrong, volunteerism is IMPORTANT, and we should all do something to make our communities better, whether it be delivering food to shut-ins, teaching Sunday school at church, serving on community committees, planning fundraisers for your schools, building homes for Habitat for Humanity, walking dogs at the Humane Society and so on. However, we should all be doing one or two things well and not taking on several things just because we can't say "No." Leaders of volunteer organizations aren't dummies; they know to ask people who won't or can't say no. It is the easiest way out to ask the same people every year. However, all our organizations would be better if we rotated in and out, bringing in fresh ideas and allowing those who have served a much-needed rest.

I served on my school system's Board of Education for ten years. In hindsight, I think I served maybe three or four years too many. It is an easy position to get jaded in since you don't have as much control over factors as you wish you would due to state guidelines and employee unions. There is never enough money, and you can't make everyone happy. I did what I could while I was there, but once I got tired of hearing complaints about athletic coaches every week (Why do we care more about sports than education?), I knew I had completed what I could in this organization. I now needed to move on to areas where I could utilize my passion for education in more meaningful and rewarding ways. Thus, I now volunteer to judge entrepreneurship competitions at the schools, to mentor business students and to give free tutoring to anyone who needs help with writing papers. By eliminating the Board of Education, I can do all these things plus write a book about things I learned in the last 20 years of being a landlord. (Check out the book on my website at www.askthelandlady or Amazon: *Lessons from the Landlady: How to Avoid My Mistakes and Be Successful in Real Estate*.) It has been fulfilling to share my knowledge and still have time to complete my life goal of writing and publishing a book. If I had continued down the path of saying "Yes" to every community organization, I would have eventually been stretched too thin. I have learned to now say, "sorry my dance card is full," when faced with a request to serve in an area that I know will not achieve a meaningful result for me or for the organization.

Create a Tickler File or 43 Folders® System

A tickler file is a system that is intended to "tickle" your memory so that important tasks get done. A tickler file has its origins in law offices in the 20th century that kept important daily and monthly files so that the office could keep track of important dates to file trademarks, briefs, motions, and other legal issues. The tickler system is also called "43 folders" by productivity experts like David Allen and Merlin Mann who write about and advocate its usage for staying on schedule. The system has 43 files: 31 daily files (less for some months, of course) and 12 monthly files for the year. To create the system, you have a prominent place where you keep the neatly arranged files and inside each file you put bills that need paid, birthday reminders, prescription refills, concert tickets, vacation plans, subscription, or professional license renewals, etc.

Each day, you pull out the file and complete the tasks inside. If you don't finish a task, you then put it into the next day file. Near the end of the month, you pull out the next monthly file and file those tasks into the daily ones. To achieve success with this method, you have to get into the important habit of consulting your tickler file each morning so you can complete the tasks. You can simply add in index cards with written reminders for monthly or seasonal tasks like changing furnace filters and watering plants. For those of you who eschew paper systems, you might want to check out the FortyThree.me app or website for a fully digital version of the technique.

I utilize a modified 43 files system for my own real estate business. Instead of 43 files, my property manager uses a binder of cheat sheets with the same concept, where each bill and due date is listed so my manager can ensure that the items are paid in a timely manner and recorded in QuickBooks. We print the list every month so that she can utilize the sheet as a checklist to stay on task. My manager also has some monthly and yearly lists with items like reminders to change furnace filters, clean drains, rake leaves to curb, and pay property taxes, yearly occupancy fees and state LLC payments. We get reminders from suppliers and agencies, but this system allows us to look ahead to budget and prepare for upcoming payments and tasks.

I have also incorporated a tickler file system with my paper calendar. I simply paperclip concert tickets and vacation plans to the corresponding months. At the beginning of the year, I write down all important birthdays and anniversaries in my new calendar, so I'm not surprised on the day of the event and realize that I have dropped the ball on sending a card or planning a special celebration. I also take the time to write out all flight confirmation numbers for ease in checking into flights and record seasonal tasks so I can look ahead and plan for their completion. In addition, I cross reference everything with my phone calendar by utilizing alerts so that I don't miss important dates or appointments.

This system is great for tracking items that happen every month or year and that are easy to overlook. For example, you might know that your real estate license needs to be renewed every three years in June, but it sure is easy to come up on that deadline and realize that you still need six continuing education credits and come up with a hefty payment to reapply. Remind your schedule-challenged family members of big events and help them set reminders periodically in the months preceding the deadline so that they don't end up missing important things. If missing deadlines is a chronic problem, help your people make a filing system that will keep track of important paperwork along with the necessary completion dates.

This is a good time to assist everyone with creating a system for dealing with important documents. After all, children will leave the home and need to know how to keep track of their birth certificates, social security cards, car titles, house deeds and passports. Teach them now how to scan documents into files for their computer as back-up and how to protect documents in fire-safe lock boxes.

Figure Out a Way to Deal with Your In-Box

While some productivity experts swear by 43 folders and other reminder systems to complete daily tasks and move forward on goals, I think your world view of your in-box is probably more complicated than so-called experts will admit. Your daily in-box might be comprised of emails, social media messages, text messages, voicemails, and physical paperwork for both work and personal usage. Thus, you must operate in both digital and physical realms, read various material, and take meaningful action. Easier said than done!

Productivity experts postulate that you must put everything into daily files and "empty" said files each day. In fact, Merlin Mann, founder of *43folders.com*, coined the productivity method "in box zero," a system where you read and empty your email box DAILY to free up your mental space to deal with more important issues. Mann's theory is that our in-box operates as a huge stressor on our lives with a huge number of divergent messages that weigh upon our time as we attempt to dredge through all the noise. Furthermore, we are often distracted every few moments by another digital alert of an incoming message that will distract us from our real work. I must admit that when I look at my husband's phone and see his message bubble say "5768" messages, I feel anxiety on his behalf. He, however, is as happy as a lark and doesn't worry about the number. Of course, he also misses many important emails which is why when he has important projects, he gives people my email address. Know yourself; if you are NEVER going to tame your email in-box, tell people to call you directly or utilize another form of communication. Or you can delegate all emails to someone who will do it for you, like a paid assistant. I do not recommend my husband's technique as it has caused me to forward emails to him with big frowny faces for taking up my time with his projects. I did, however, take time to clean up his in-box one time with folders and deletions to help him get back on track. This is something you can do for your ADHD and organizationally challenged family members to reduce everyone's stress and get everyone on a better system. Or if everything in the in-box is out of date, delete it all and start over!

You also might also decrease the avenues in which people can communicate to your schedule-challenged person. If emails are out of control, don't let people send them to you, or create a message that bounces back saying that emails are not read and to instead use an alternative form of communication. In fact, my husband used to get so many phone calls with his job that he created a voicemail message telling people to NOT leave a message since he would never listen to the recording and to—instead—send a text message which he would see, read, and respond to.

In his productivity blogs, Merlin Mann advocates a process for the in-box where you check it two to three times per day and then employ a four-step process to Delete, Delegate, Defer or Do each item. To accomplish this system, you need to create folders for all your in-box venues for your deferred items or things that you need to save. I recently tried out this system for my email boxes because, although I go through my email daily and get things done, the messages were still defeating me at times. I take the time to religiously unsubscribe and delete advertising emails to keep that wolf at bay. However, I have noticed that if I skip a few days, those emails get out of control quickly! I know one technique is to use one specific email address for all purchases so that you can ignore that email box altogether. However, I have found that I often must search for an email to find an order number or to track a package, especially around the holidays. I regularly operate among four email addresses, three of them for business ventures and one for personal usage. Over the years, the system has gotten muddy as I've used different emails for cross purposes, so now, I really do have to keep tabs on all four boxes. Luckily my iPhone makes that easy; however, there are still a lot of messages to track. Thus, I created several folders and took an hour to assign all my saved in-box emails to these different folders: Vacation Plans, Real Estate Work, Medical Billing Work, Book Contacts, and Personal Stuff. I made sure to only pick a handful of topics so the filing of each email would be quick and effortless. After working with this system for a couple of days, I do have to say that I like having a streamlined in-box where messages do not get overwhelming. For this system to be successful, though, I am going to have to take the time to periodically delete items in my folders that are no longer relevant so the folders themselves do not become too overwhelming.

Merlin Mann and other productivity experts say that you should NOT use your email as a To-Do list. However, I have found that for the nature of my work, even after deleting, delegating, and deferring, I still leave the last few messages intact as my to-do list. Sometimes I am away from my laptop and the tasks that need to be completed are more easily accomplished when I am seated at my desk and using a bigger screen. In fact, I pull up websites and leave them hanging up there on my smartphone as reminders as well, like recipes I need to make, books I want to request from the library and research ideas for my businesses and books. So, while the compiling and organizing techniques work to reduce stress, I still utilize my in-box and my internet browser as to-do lists of items that I need to refer to and work on within the next two days. After that time, I will finish the tasks or assign them to the folders. This will simply always be an area of my life where I defy the productivity gurus; this usage of technology works well for me, so I see no need to change my system.

For some people, physical mail might even be a time management issue. I have visited friends who have an overwhelming mountain of envelopes in their kitchen that would make me break out in hives. And I know some retirees that regularly flit between houses and get so much mail that the post office starts refusing envelopes because they won't fit in the P.O. boxes, causing havoc when important mail arrives for their business enterprises. Luckly, there are a few different techniques you can use here. You can opt into all digital correspondence to save trees and to move everything away from the physical mailbox—a particularly great option if you travel often. Also, you can contact each supplier directly and ask them to either stop sending you information or use an email address. There are also some online websites that will help you decrease advertising material. The Federal Trade Commission recommends that consumers use the Association of National Advertiser's website (www.ana.net) to unsubscribe from all advertising lists. At the time of this book's publication there is a nominal fee of $4-$5 dollars to eliminate much of your junk mail.

The in-box is a complicated system for all of us and there really is no one way to solve the problem for your other family members. **However, there are several ideas that will reduce stress and increase productivity.** You might try some of these methods with them:

- Only check your in-box and social media messages two or three times daily, not all throughout the day. Turn off notifications so the alerts do not interfere with your other daily activities, giving you much needed peace when relaxing and helping you to stay focused when studying or working.

- Create folders for the in-box that make sense for the in-box owner. However, do not create too many folders; the filing system needs to be quick and intuitive, or it will fail.

- Consider out-sourcing the organization phase to someone else just to jumpstart the process and motivate the disorganized person to seek better habits. ADHD individuals will have difficulty deciding which folders to create, so find a trusted, organized person (maybe you!) to help them get on track.

- Periodically review your system, further deleting files and unsubscribing from mailing lists to get your in-box items streamlined and under control.

- Do what works for you. If emails get lost, ask everyone to call or text you. If you hate handling paper copies, have everything sent digitally to you to review on your laptop or smartphone. If your in-box stays full for several days but you are still highly productive, ignore the experts who say that the box should be emptied each day.

Deploy a Body Doubling or Mirroring Technique

Many ADHD resources mention the excellent results that people are having with utilizing a body doubling technique. Body doubling is when you have another person around while you perform a task. That person doesn't need to be actively helping you with the task but he or she is there to provide support and focus. I already discussed how my daughter Isabelle just likes to have me or a friend with her while she sorts through her clothing. I can simply sit there drinking my tea or answering emails. Isabelle likes the physical presence to help her stay present and motivated to finish her task. She knows that if she quits halfway, I will gently prompt her. If she gets stuck, she can ask her friend to help her figure out if it is time to donate her pink sweatshirt or if it still looks good enough to wear. For this system to work well, the body double must be aware that the person working is trying to actively finish a task. Thus, the body double will not add to the distraction but provide a calming presence.

My sister-in-law, Jamie, and I were recently walking with another friend. On the walk, Jamie mentioned that she had her kids carry all the Christmas stuff to the attic, but here it was February, and the decorations were all still sitting there. Jamie said she needed to get it packed up and put away but just couldn't seem to get it done. Our friend just looked at Jamie and said, "well, just go up there and do it." Jamie and I laughed and laughed because with our extensive experience and research with ADHD, we knew that "just do it" wasn't such an easy option for her (even though Nike has made billions telling us that same thing for years!). However, having this discussion gave Jamie resolve; she called her mother and asked her to come over and visit. Jamie knew that her mother would tell her to put it away and sit with her having coffee while the task got done.

Experts say that body doubling is not just for people with ADHD and that everyone can benefit from the social presence that makes tasks more joyful simply by having human contact. In fact, body doubling works great on tasks that are unpleasant, like cleaning and doing yard work. Some people prefer to listen to music or listen to a book or podcast, but having someone with you can make the task more palatable, even if you don't talk or engage in the same activity. Body doubling helps reduce social isolation and provides necessary support and motivation to keep working. Research has shown this works well even in pursuits that we consider to be solitary, like studying for a big test or completing paperwork. To help motivate your kids to finish homework, simply park them in the room with you while you cook dinner or perform another task. Just having a human presence increases accountability and motivation.

If no one is around to be the body double, you can also try mirroring through watching videos of other people trying to do the same task. Mirroring differs from body doubling because the person who has difficulty with focus and attention will "mirror" or copy the actions of the other person. ADHD people who have difficulty with figuring out social cues and have anxiety in outings with other friends often use mirroring to help "fit in" and improve social interactions. You are probably already familiar with mirroring through workout classes, where you watch someone else work out and try to copy their actions. People have simply applied this mirroring to other tasks, like cleaning the house and crafting. There are a lot of TikTok and YouTube videos where you can see this technique in action. If no one is around to help you organize your closet, you can pull up a YouTube video of other people organizing their clothing and be inspired to continue working and finish your task. If you are procrastinating on finishing a knitting project, you can pull up a video of someone else knitting and simply knit along with him or her. This works very well on tasks that you are unsure of how to perform— to learn as you go and to be motivated to start difficult jobs and stay on task. One YouTube channel you might want to check out is @DianaADHD; Diana is a life coach who performs household tasks like ironing clothes, folding laundry, and washing dishes where she encourages you to do the same task while you watch/listen to her do the same work.

FaceTime is also a great tool to utilize for both body doubling and mirroring. If your ADHD person needs to work on homework and no one is available at home, he or she can FaceTime with someone else. The FaceTime friend can be working on the same homework or on another type of paperwork. Just that presence of another person working can be the impetus needed for your ADHD person to stay motivated and follow through on his or her task. Many content creators on TikTok and YouTube are also starting to replicate the FaceTime style of speaking to their audience in a more collegial, friendly manner which also provides that needed sense of companionship.

Institute a Set Weekly Family Routine

In the last chapter I discussed fulfilling daily, incremental tasks as one of the techniques your family could employ to establish good organizational habits. This is where you would empty the dishwasher every morning or pick up the living room each night. However, there is something to be said behind the old household mantra: "Wash on Monday, Iron on Tuesday, Mend on Thursday, Churn on Thursday, Clean on Friday, Bake on Saturday and Rest on Sunday." There is no need to reinvent the wheel after all, so if this type of system works for you and your family—do it! This is a particularly good technique for people who have difficulty with cyclical tasks like laundry and cleaning that have no end points. Doing these activities daily might cause more anxiety than simply doing them once per week. Thus, choose the night when everyone is home to do laundry tasks. And make cleaning happen on Saturday afternoon before everyone wants to go out to their friends' houses or to the movies. Instead, use daily tasks to do more self-help activities like exercise, meditate, journal, or connect with other family members. You may even be more efficient this way, since a focused session of cleaning or meal prep saves you from the daily distractions of these activities that might take away from more important life goals. If your house stays orderly overall, there is no problem with letting dishes pile up a couple of days before you tackle them on Thursday night when everyone has more free time because there is no soccer practice or youth group meeting. The key here is to have a time set aside when the task will get completed and to make sure there is follow-through.

Keep a running project list

Let's face it. You will never run out of stuff to do. When I first started my business, I hired independent contractors who worked by the hour to complete apartment turnovers. Basically, we would go through the apartment and make a list of everything that needed to be done, like performing basic maintenance, adding upgrades, cleaning, and painting. After a while I started to notice how the contractors would start to drag their feet on the last couple days of the job. I would be itching to get the apartment rented and the workers would be stalling or slowing the job down. When I confronted them about the situation, the workers admitted that they were worried about running out of work. Well! That worry was easily remedied. I assured them that when you own property, you never run out of work. There was always something that needed painted, cleaned, weeded, upgraded, or fixed. We started to keep a running project list so I could employ the workers full time with the goal that they would finish apartments in a timely manner, and on down periods, work on the projects like power washing, porch painting, etc.

It is easy to keep a project list. You can type it into the notes section of your smartphone, write it on a whiteboard, list it in your planner or keep an entire journal of ideas and projects for the future. I like the journal idea because I can list out mundane aspects but also keep great ideas that hit me at different times that I might want to pursue in the future. I recently got my husband to adopt the system because he was constantly spouting off different ideas and then telling me to help him remember them. Since it is hard enough to remember my own stuff, I got him a beautiful notebook and told him to write down the ideas himself. Now when he is hit with an epiphany about a new iPhone medical app or cool art project, he can jot it down in the notebook and have all these ideas in one place.

I like putting things in my journal that are wish lists for the future. For example, I have a dream of organizing all my smart phone photographs into digital albums and erasing all the extraneous photos I no longer need, like pictures of shoes I wanted to purchase or books that I wanted to read, not to mention all the duplicate photographs cluttering up the phone. I have not yet gotten around to that project, but it is listed in my journal. Now when I have some time to kill, I will remember that task better simply because I wrote it down as a future project that I wanted to tackle. I also write down books that I want to read in the future and quilting projects that I would like to complete.

To sum up, there are several different ways to get your family into better routines and to motivate them to complete tasks and goals. Try out different techniques yourself and with family members to see what has a lasting impact. Consider what electronic tools and old school methods work best. Don't assume that everyone works well with technological methods. Some people may prefer to use pencil and paper, index cards or even an old-fashioned rolodex. When I implemented a software program for my real estate business, our office was empowered; this program revolutionized the way we tracked rents, accepted applications, received work orders, and completed background checks. Our maintenance staff, however, was not impressed. In fact, one of my long-term guys (who still calls me "Kid"), said that the day I made him carry around an iPad to do work orders was the day he would quit and not look back. The rest of the guys nodded in agreement. Message received! In the office, we simply adapted and created a system that worked for the maintenance workers. We print off the work orders, prioritize them and highlight all pertinent notes like, "Don't go in until after 10:00 am," or "Don't let the cat out." The guys now carry around clipboards to hold the papers and simply write their notes directly onto each sheet. Every day they drop off the work orders with any receipts and we take over from there, updating the computer system and filing all the receipts. We all have different mindsets and different skill sets; this is why no ONE way will work for your entire family or workforce.

CHAPTER 8
CHEAT SHEET

Here are thirteen different strategies to consider with your family members:

1   **Maintain Multiple Calendars.**

    Keep old school paper calendars and smartphone calendars so that you can see a global vision as well as a daily snapshot of events.

2   **Create and Maintain ONE Family Calendar.**

    Put this calendar where EVERYONE can see it and post important information and events.

3   **Develop Personalized Reminder Systems.**

    Consider your family members' personalities and organizational approaches and come up with individual reminders that help each person. Try out different ideas like whiteboards, chalkboards, post-it notes, index cards, digital reminders, smartphone alerts, running lists and imaginary deadlines. See what sticks and continuously improve upon the process.

4   **Create Specific Prompts.**

    Talk to your family members about the best prompts to remind them of important tasks. Utilize behavioral, visual, and vocal prompts to assist yourself and others to get from task to task or to help decrease bad habits and implement good ones in their place.

5 **Consider Utilizing the Pomodoro Technique.**

   Help people stay FOCUSED by establishing 25-minute intervals of focused work followed by five-minute breaks. Remove distractions and obstacles while the focused work is in process. Make sure to take the breaks to build in some enjoyment and self-care.

6 **Do the Hardest Task First.**

   Tackle the scary and eat the frog. Encourage your procrastinators to do that one HARD task first thing in the morning and then reward themselves afterwards with screen time, a snack, a relaxing bath, or any other de-stress activity before going on with the rest of the day. Tell them it is time to just start already and to take action. However, it is still important to remember that reward process to reinforce the behavior!

7 **Break Tasks Down into a Step-by-Step Process.**

   Help your ADHD and other focus-challenged family members to break down hard goals into smaller, more manageable tasks. You can utilize artificial intelligence or just some planning time to chunk out into smaller goals.

8 **Eliminate Busy Work from Your Daily Routine.**

   Audit the family and find the time wasters and busy work activities that keep everyone from fulfilling goals and enjoying life. Refine, outsource, or eliminate activities that are just bringing everyone down so that your family can be more achievement-oriented and have more time to spend together doing fun things. Embrace change.

9 **Create a Tickler File or 43 Folders® System.**

   Help everyone find a way to remember important tasks that occur in the future, like renewing licenses, applying for benefits, performing seasonal household tasks and more. Figure out a way for everyone to learn how to file important papers.

10 Figure Out a Way to Deal with Your In-Box.

This can be complicated but take the time to talk about all the options. There is no best way to solve the issue of constant, incoming information. If your family members lack focus, help them find the best avenue for receiving messages. Then, have your people announce that communication line to everyone, cutting off the avenues that your family members will not check, read, or respond to in a timely fashion. As the organized one of the family, help them create a filing or organizational system for all their incoming messages and information.

11 Deploy a Body Doubling or Mirroring Technique.

Asking someone to sit with you while you do work or copying someone while they do tasks are both great options for everyone to employ. While many in the ADHD community have championed these techniques as ways to get motivated and stay on task, experts say that both have their utility for everyone because humans often work better together instead of in isolation.

12 Institute a Set Weekly Family Routine.

If incremental daily items just don't work for your crew, set up tasks for once a week or once a month to increase efficiency and help everyone carve out the time needed to achieve personal goals and aspirations.

13 Keep a Running Project List.

Write down big ideas for the future so that you don't forget them. Give your creative ideas the attention they deserve!

(9)

LET'S MAKE THIS FUN

As I have noted in previous chapters, I think that rewards are important for everyone. I am not of the belief that we all deserve a trophy or gold medal, but when an onerous task gets completed, I think celebrations are in order. For some tasks, like cleaning out the closets before shopping sprees and organizing the bedrooms before birthdays and holidays, the reward is, ironically, the ability to acquire more stuff! However, you could find some other motivations, particularly after long days spent cleaning basements and garages, like ordering pizza or going to the movies. Holding a yard sale will result in cash which seems to be a good motivator for everyone. And we have already discussed how rewards work better than consequences when trying to motivate chronic procrastinators.

But not every day can be a party and some tasks are just totally sucky, like cleaning out an apartment when someone must go into a nursing home or helping a friend get rid of his deceased spouse's clothing. Those might be more grit your teeth and get it done tasks. They are also excellent tasks to share with close friends or siblings. If it is extremely emotional, consider hiring someone to pack everything up. Your mental well-being is more important than spending hours going through stuff. You can simply pull-out important items or list them for someone else to find for you.

When it comes to just regular decluttering and organizing, you can do a few other things to make it more palatable to your family. For young children, you can make pick up into a time game by setting a five-minute timer on your phone and urging your kids to work as fast as possible to beat the timer. For your significant other or older kids, you can save up juicy stories to talk everyone through difficult tasks. I have a workout teacher, Debbie, who will chat away about local town news just to distract her class from the grueling four-minute planks or other abuse she is inflicting on us at the moment, and it works! Before you know it, the hard exercise is completed, the living room is dusted, or the dishes are washed and put away.

Once you finish the monumental task of going through everything in a room, removing trash and unused items and organizing your most important items, then a great reward can be those fun containers and display cabinets that you have seen on TikTok and at Hobby Lobby. (Finally, we got there!) It's also important to recognize and applaud the milestones that your family members achieve along the way to reaching their goals. Don't just celebrate graduation from college, but make sure you celebrate all the milestones, like great midterm grades, praise from professors and interest in college coursework. We all need praise and positive feedback to feel good about ourselves and to motivate us to stay on the path, especially when it gets rocky and difficult.

And don't forget to high five yourself when you get things done. This is a good way to motivate others. If they see you finishing a task and THEN rewarding yourself with a hot bath, a cup of tea or 30 minutes of television, then your family might just jump on this delayed gratification train with you.

I'm going to sound like a grouchy old person here on my soapbox, but technology has provided all of us with too many opportunities to avoid hard work. Researchers have studied how online shopping, scrolling through social media, and playing video games can all contribute to releases of dopamine in our brains. Dopamine is the neurotransmitter hormone that makes us feel good and makes us continuously seek that feel-good sensation. Of course, sucky work tasks do not contribute to our dopamine level, so we often seek the easy way out to avoid boring or hard tasks and instead, gravitate towards other activities that make us feel good.

In her book, *Dopamine Nation: Finding Balance in the Age of Indulgence*, Dr. Anna Lembke, a Stanford psychiatrist, postulates that due to the proliferation of abundant distractions, humans might no longer get enjoyment out of simpler tasks. For example, people who play a lot of video games might get addicted to the constant dopamine rushes from gaming and eschew the opportunity to sit at the kitchen table with the family playing a game of Yahtzee. Other scientists caution that the dopamine issue is more complicated and might involve a myriad of factors. For example, drug addictions have other issues; you cannot compare the rush of dopamine that individuals get from drugs like cocaine with the dopamine increase from a session of online shopping. In any case, scientists agree that current research does support the idea that our attention span has been significantly shortened by our constant interaction with digital interfaces like social media, texts, emails, and videos. To be productive and keep focus, we must learn how to manage these technologies and still stay engaged and enjoy the fun aspects of all of these distractions. One good way to accomplish this task is to stay unplugged for set periods of time to get tasks done and then tie our reward to a set amount of time afterwards to do our gaming, texting, or social media scrolling.

CHAPTER 9
CHEAT SHEET

- Reward yourself and others whenever you can to reinforce jobs well done and to validate good habits.

- Use your stress-relieving, distracting activities as rewards AFTER work is completed.

- Look—you have made it through nine chapters of this book on dealing with chaotic homes and different family opinions—HIGH FIVE!

- You have learned a lot of strategies that might make a difference in your home and hopefully got a boost of motivation for change.

(10)

SHOW ME THE MONEY

I have already discussed how yard sales can be a great way to get rid of stuff, especially your larger items like furniture, sporting gear, exercise equipment and basically anything else that you would rather not have to haul away. Note, however, that this might not include pianos. In fact, my neighbors had to hire someone to remove an upright piano for them after offering it to people for "free if you come pick it up" for several months.

In addition to yard sales, there are several other options for making money and unloading your stuff. However, there are some things to consider when making the decision to sell items.

1. **Does the item have value?**

    This can be very subjective. Some people, like my husband, think their items have tremendous value even when others look at the stuff and consider them trash. Therefore, it might be a good idea to have a third party or two look at your stuff and help you determine if your item is worth finding another outlet. In your family you can make a selling plan with a deadline. For us, this means we hold two yard sales while also posting items on social media.

Whatever does not sell gets donated after the second yard sale. Having that hard deadline is particularly important for those of you who want to drag your feet on unloading stuff. However, items with more intrinsic value to collectors and other people willing to pay higher prices will need to be listed online to get a bigger audience.

2   **Are the items small enough to ship?**

Small items can be advertised on eBay or other online sites and sold to a worldwide audience, possibly garnering a higher profit. However, your couch is going to be more easily sold to someone who will come to pick it up from your home. Shipping will require you to package up everything carefully and utilize the postal system or UPS to ship. Online sales venues like eBay and Mercari will let you print postal labels at home which definitely makes the process easier. However, you will have to account for packing tape and shipping materials in your price point. Since we sell a lot of items on eBay, my husband and I have put out an all-call to our friends asking them to save packing boxes and shipping material like bubble wrap and brown paper. With everyone buying things online all the time, this is pretty easy. My friends are happy to recycle their packing material and boxes and I don't have to pay for these materials which will affect my profit margin.

3   **Do you have the ability and patience to sell your own items?**

It is not easy work to post all your items online or even in person. If you are selling online, you must take pictures and write good, accurate descriptions of all your items. If you are selling in person, you must be free to meet with people to make the sale. At one point in time, I enlisted all my kids in a packing and shipping operation in my dining room to run our eBay enterprise. So, you must have the space to store your items while selling and stay organized enough to find the objects, pack them carefully and mail them to the buyers. If staying organized and running around shipping items is not your forte or your interest, then you might want to find another way to dispose of unwanted items, like donating or asking someone else to sell for you with a commission.

4 Are you legally able to sell the item?

Online sites have items that they restrict for sale purposes due to ethical or legal concerns, so you want to be aware of these prohibitions. For example, we ended up with some real photo antique postcards of Hitler from the early 1930s that were in a home we purchased to tear down (weird, I know!). In any case, eBay did not allow us to post these; they have some historic value to collectors but are considered "hate speech" items (rightly so! I just wanted these awful things out of my house). You might also want to be careful if you have items that are counterfeit or fake, like designer purses, clothing, and jewelry. If you are unsure, make sure that you reveal that uncertainty in your descriptions, so you are not accused of passing along fraudulent items.

There are several venues to consider for selling items. Here are some you might want to try for unloading your stuff:

- **Yard sales are a great way to do a one-day cleanup of your clutter.**

If your neighborhood does a yearly yard sale, it is a no-brainer. There will be a lot of foot traffic for a collective sale that involves several households. If you have a sunny day, you will ensure a good crowd. This is perfect for unloading a lot of household items, clothing and other general items that are not high-end or highly valued. At the end of the sale, you can simply pack up the rest and donate it all, or you can offer it on Facebook Marketplace to someone for cheap or free if they come and pick up all the stuff.

- **Facebook Marketplace is a great option for unloading large items at your convenience.**

    First, it is FREE. Second, it lets you reach your local customer base, which is particularly helpful for getting rid of big, heavy items that cannot easily be shipped. Third, once that person comes to see your dining room table, they might be persuaded to also purchase that set of shelves you are trying to unload. Also, you will get quick cash in hand for not a lot of effort, and you get to set the meeting time and place. If you don't want people to come to your home, then meet them at a public parking lot. If you have large items, arrange for your burly neighbor or another friend to be home with you. Drag the item outside so that you will not have to invite strangers into your home. When listing items on Facebook, you can cross-reference several local yard sale, buy/sell/trade, or bulletin board sites to reach a wide audience. However, be aware of popular scams that involve people trying to pay with Zello or Venmo. I simply tell people I only accept cash to steer clear of any issues. Personal checks can bounce, so don't accept those either. Also, do not give out your personal phone number or any other secure information. Stay on the platform; some unscrupulous people will try to entice you to give out your phone number and jump off the platform to perform some sort of scam. If you sense a red flag, report the potential buyer to the internet platform, and move on to someone else.

- **eBay is the premier place for collectible, smaller items.**

    If you have coins, jewelry, dolls, vintage items, artwork, etc, then eBay is a great place to reach a worldwide audience, especially if you are willing to ship overseas. eBay's rules change all the time, but basically you get to list up to 200 items free per month for public auction or buy it now features. After that, each listing incurs a fee of 35 cents. Depending on the sales category, eBay takes a percentage, usually 3 percent commission along with an extra charge of 30 cents per item. If the item goes up for auction, you set a price and the listing has 7 days for buyers to make bids. This is the best way to go for hot ticket items that you know will get some competition. The buy it now feature is better served for items like books, clothing that is new with tags and other items that might need to sit for a month or two to get noticed in a search. With the buy it now feature, you get to set the specific sales price. In addition, you can add an option that allows potential buyers to make an offer. For example, you might list a coat for $25.00 and someone after a month or two might come along with a $20 offer. You will have 24 hours to accept, reject or counteroffer. Things to keep in mind with eBay include packaging items, printing postage labels and going to the post office. If you want items gone quickly, you are better off starting with a yard sale or offering on social media sites. However, if you want to make a little more money and don't mind waiting a bit, this is a valid option. That $20 coat probably would only garner $10 or less at a yard sale or on local social media sites. Over the years, eBay has gotten technologically fancy. After uploading pictures and typing in a heading, the application will assist you in writing up a description. Honestly, the artificial intelligence employed here is pretty accurate! This is a huge time saver if you plan to post several items for auction or sale.

To save time and money on postage, I always use the eBay postage feature. When you list the items, plan out the box or packaging and weigh the item so that the website can more accurately predict shipping. You can also look at other people's listings of the same item to see what they charge for shipping and utilize their numbers. Or you can build the cost into your price and offer free shipping which is often very attractive to your buyers who are used to Amazon prime shipping. If you have a computer at home, you can simply purchase shipping and print paper labels to tape to your packaging which is a huge time saver. Also, you get a little bit of a break in shipping this way which accounts for your "handling" costs of packing tape, printing paper, and dropping boxes to the post office. If you have a lot of items, you can even schedule a pickup with your local post office. To save money on mailers and boxes, simply ask your friends and neighbors to recycle their packing materials by giving them all to you. With everyone online shopping all the time, there should be no need to purchase packing materials unless you really go to town with online selling, or you have very strangely shaped items.

- **Mercari, Poshmark and The RealReal are great venues for clothing, shoes, and fashion accessories.**

  If you have a lot of name brand and designer clothing, especially geared towards the younger crowd, then these three websites are great places to check out for online selling. They have easy apps to navigate and will send you prepaid shipping labels to make the process easier. These apps make their money from the commission which varies from a flat rate for cheaper items to a 20 percent commission. If you plan to sell a lot of items, research each site to see who has the best terms. Sometimes they run specials to get you in as a seller as well.

- **Auctions are a great place to liquidate furniture, house items and collections.**

  Check out your local auction house and see what percentage the auctioneers charge. In my town, the auctioneers will take just a few items to join in with larger auctions or will sell an entire household. Auction houses also often have transportation and personnel available to come pick up heavy items. This is a great option for antiques, collectibles, and nice furniture.

- **Trading venues are another option for people who have a lot of collectibles or hobby items.**

    Of course, this means you are not really getting rid of items, but it does mean you are curating them, so that things you don't need are being traded for items that you can use or that fit a certain hobby or collection. Your area might have a swap meet or flea market where you can barter items or even set up a table to liquidate your stuff.

There is a proliferation of other internet sites and applications that will hit niche audiences.

A simple internet search will alert you to websites that might best suit your needs or websites that better serve your locale. In large cities, apps take the place of social media listings and will provide you with better security. If you have specialized athletic gear or trendy furniture, you will probably get more traction on some of the niche websites available.

Another item to keep in mind about selling your items is tax reporting. If the total amount sold on any internet platform exceeds $600, then that website is required to issue you a 1099-K form that you will have to report on your annual taxes. Therefore, you will need to keep good records of your costs, like packing materials, postage, and transportation costs in order to mitigate this line item on your taxes. You can even set up a business that will provide you with some other tax benefits if you plan to do this often.

And of course, if online selling just seems too time consuming and annoying, you can look at some other venues like local consignment shops where you can drop off your items and have the stores sell the items for you and take a cut of the proceeds. You will get some money for the items and in the end, everything can be donated. Or simply take everything to a local thrift store and receive receipts to deduct the donation from your yearly taxes.

CHAPTER 10 CHEAT SHEET

Questions to ask yourself about items you want to sell:
- Does the item have value?
- Is the item easy to ship?
- Do you have the ability and patience to sell your items?
- Are you legally able to sell the item?

Possible Selling Venues:
- Yard sales
- Facebook Marketplace and other social media sites
- eBay and other online auctions
- Mercari, Poshmark and the RealReal for clothing and fashion accessories
- Auction houses
- Trading sites, flea markets and swap meets

(11)

DEALING WITH DIFFICULT ORGANIZATIONAL SITUATIONS

We have gone through ten chapters focused on gently prodding your chaotic family towards better systems of organization. However, there are some super difficult situations that might have you feeling angry, bitter, or just plain sad. I get it. Organizing doesn't just comprise systems of dividing your bookshelves into the colors of the rainbow and matching up all the socks in the laundry room. We are humans and we behave like it. And situations like divorce, downsizing, moving, going to a nursing home and death make the organization process much more stressful.

After passing the 80-year age mark, Margareta Magnusson decided to write an organizational book that has been all the rage on social media. In her book, *The Gentle Art of Swedish Death Cleaning*, Magnusson describes a Swedish concept where people remove all unnecessary items and make their homes nice and orderly before death. As she states in her book, women are usually the ones who shoulder the burden of death cleaning since they are often the primary homemakers, they live longer and they already cleanup after the family on a daily basis. Magnusson postulates that adults should start the process of death cleaning around age 65 to reduce the burden for other family members. While no one really wants to use the D word—(stage whisper: "death")—it is a good idea to start talking your elderly loved ones about their stuff. We all know horror stories about families turning into vultures after the funeral, coming in and pillaging the family home for treasures. So why not talk to your family now to reduce the stress later?

If your family members can easily talk about impending death, then ask them to tag their prized possessions or list them in the will so the items will go to their intended beneficiaries. I have always been haunted by a story my grandmother told me about visiting her sick mother in the hospital. My great-grandmother wanted to give my grandmother the rings off her fingers because she knew she was facing death. My grandmother said, "No, Mother, I cannot stand to see your fingers without your beautiful rings." Well, flashforward a few days later and the wives of my grandmother's loser brothers had all pilfered the rings and my grandmother never got any of the jewelry—even though that was not the original intention.

Instead, heed the example of my mother-in-law, Phyllis, who has already passed down some of her prized possessions to grandchildren who have admired them. She packed up all her holiday dishes to give to one granddaughter and packed up beautiful tablecloths for another grandchild. It has made her very happy to see and know that these objects are going to family members who will cherish them.

Recently my youngest daughter, Isabelle, and I visited my mum, Janet, who is a prolific and talented knitter. My daughter asked her grandma if she had any knitted creations sitting around that Isabelle could take back to college in snowy Colorado. My mum directed Isabelle to her wardrobe and told her to take whatever she wanted. When I protested that Isabelle should not pilfer everything, my mum said, "I'm 78. When people come to my house and want something, they are going to go home with it." This is a great attitude towards sharing your stuff with the next generation.

Ironically, it is the more mundane objects and stuff that can cause emotional distress with older family members, especially if these objects represent a downsizing or move to an assisted living home. My friend Jan recently told me about her experience in helping her parents hold a yard sale with stuff that came from the basement of a house they wanted to sell. Her parents hired household help to pack up everything and transport it to my friend's garage. Imagine her dismay, when Jan looked at the stuff and realized it was mostly bric-a-brac and dated decorative items from the 1980s. There were even a couple of broken-down small appliances. She didn't want any of it and didn't see much hope in getting any money out of the stuff. However, her parents were adamant about trying a sale because the stuff was expensive back in the day, and they couldn't fathom throwing away items that had cost so much. Jan was not optimistic about the whole situation but felt compelled to make her parents happy. Thus, she woke up early on a Friday morning to get everything out for the sale. Since she had to work that day, she hired someone to help her elderly parents conduct the sale, with the understanding that everything would be packed up and donated at the end.

At the end of her working shift, Jan came home to the piles of stuff still in her garage. After a disappointing sale day of just $31.25, her parents insisted on keeping half of the items to try to sell again back in their town. To add insult to injury, the remainder of the items had still not been taken to the donation site because her parents preferred a different donation location that was 20 minutes further away. Jan was angry and disappointed. She had a long day at work and had thought that a clear plan was in place. She had even paid people to make sure the plan would succeed. But, of course, these were her parents whom she loved and respected. There was no getting around it. Jan paid her helper, spent her Friday evening transporting all the donated items to the new site and helped her parents pack the remaining items back into their car. When Jan relayed the story to me the next day, she told me she felt defeated because her careful plan had failed. "I should have just thrown everything away. My parents didn't even know what was in that basement and would never have missed anything," she lamented.

The type A personality part of me totally agreed with her. It would have been way less work to just eliminate everything at the beginning. However, her parents were sentimental souls and they wanted to see what was stored in their basement. And it was their house and their stuff. This was the day that Jan learned the lesson that she should set up clear boundaries, so this didn't happen again. After all, the stuff wasn't in her house. Jan was worried about the amount of stuff her parents were going to leave her in the future, but that didn't mean she had to act on that fear right now. Because her parents knew they had too much stuff and wanted to get their old house in order so it could eventually be sold, they were striving to please Jan and start the process of downsizing. After we talked about the situation, Jan came to a few conclusions:

- Jan could celebrate the fact that half of the items were gone, even if the process was more costly and time-consuming than expected.

- Jan realized that her parents' insistence that the items come to Jan's house was because they wanted her to look at everything with them. So now, Jan could tell her parents that she did not personally have time to help with another disappointing yard sale but that she would go to their house and look at everything with them.

- Jan could reassure her parents that they could keep whatever they wanted. However, if there was stuff that they wanted gone, Jan would help remove it—but only if the items went directly to trash or to a donation site. If there were some better items that could be sold for $50 or higher, Jan could offer to advertise on Facebook Marketplace or other social media sites.

This story highlights a couple of key points about some of the differences in our approaches to stuff:

- **For some people, especially those in older generations, the ability to get rid of items is thwarted by financial concerns.** Jan's elderly parents remembered paying a lot of money for hand painted Christmas decorations. However, like most of her generation, Jan purchased her decorative items from Home Goods, Amazon, Target, and the Dollar Tree. Items now are simply cheaper and seen as disposable. Jan's parents thought they had "investment" items that should be used every Christmas. However, those investment items, like the gold angel put on top of the tree every year and the special green goblets used for Christmas dinner were still being used by Jan's parents. Those items would be handed down to Jan eventually. However, the items in the basement, while expensive at the time, were now dated and just not useful to Jan or really anyone else, as evidenced by the fact that none of it sold at the disappointing yard sale. While we can dismiss Jan's parents' stuff as unfashionable and no longer relevant, I think we can all appreciate the fact that it is difficult to throw away or give away something that you remember paying a lot of money for at one time. Also, since fashions change and trends are often cyclical, these decorative items might actually come back into style. However, Jan and her parents had to address the fact that storing the items for just the possibility of resurgent fashion might not be feasible.

- **Some family members are more practical in their approach to stuff.** While we live in a very disposable society now, our elders remember a time when appliances lasted forty years and technicians were employed to fix everything from your toaster to your lamps. Jan's dad had several small household appliances that just needed a new screw, some cleaning, or a small part to be in working order. However, Jan's parents also had all the new household appliances and did not need these items. Furthermore, her father's health kept him from having the energy and inclination to find the parts and perform the maintenance. But since Jan's father had a lot of pride for the things he fixed over the years, it was difficult for him to part with items that he knew he could have fixed easily in his younger days. It seemed obvious to Jan that these unnecessary items were taking up space. She had to find gentle ways to tell her dad that it was okay to get rid of the items and instead spend his time on more enjoyable pursuits like doing sudoku puzzles and attending his grandson's soccer games.

- **A big clean up can be emotional since it represents the end of an era and a dismantling of goals and dreams that were established earlier in life.** In the quilting world, people talk about UFOs, or unfinished objects, which are all the projects that quilters start but never finish. There are podcasts and online support groups dedicated to motivating quilters to finish their projects. Other quilters will tell you how to organize your UFOs into piles and how to schedule time to complete the projects. These same quilters will encourage you to post progress pictures on social media sites to provide further inspiration. I have tried some of their techniques, but I have also given myself permission to give up on projects. I just chalk the unfinished Dresden plate pattern quilt up to a "skill building exercise" and simply donate it to the quilt club at my daughter's elementary school or to the local charity shop. It is okay to start projects and never finish them, especially when they are just hobbies and supposed to be fun and free of drama. When the hobby you choose to reduce your stress actually starts elevating your stress—then it is time to let go of that hobby. It is not a failure when you now hate the craft or project and just have better things to do. Inanimate objects, like unfinished quilting projects, are not children. It is perfectly fine to abandon these objects or send them somewhere else to be adopted.

All the decorations that Jan's mom had stored in her basement came from a time when she decorated her huge house for all the children. Said children now all had homes of their own and different decorating aesthetics. Removing all the decorations was emotional for Jan's mother because it hammered home the point that she no longer had the energy and desire to decorate her house in such lavish style. And the woodworking equipment that was languishing in the basement represented the notion that Jan's dad had not achieved his dream of making custom wood toys. Jan had to tread lightly in these areas because unrealized dreams and letting go of the past are hard for everyone. Jan had to remind both of her parents that their lives today were still rich and rewarding. After all, her parents had new hobbies they enjoyed, and they did not miss the hard work that their woodworking and decorating necessitated.

- **Getting rid of items can generate guilt in some of your family members.** Jan felt guilty about pushing her parents to get rid of things. She knew it was the most practical solution and that it would make moving easier, but she hated to see her parents in distress over stuff.

Some of your family members might feel guilty about getting rid of items that they knew were expensive or that were gifts from loved ones. I call this **Object Burden**. We have all received an expensive gift that we just did not care for or ever use. We cannot return the item and over time the item starts to feel like a burden. It is not practical to get out the expensive Lennox vase every time your Aunt Doris comes to visit, and the vase doesn't match any of your other décor. It's also hard to get rid of the formal winter coat that you purchased but have only worn once because it is uncomfortable and impractical. That coat represents an impulsive, bad purchase and the mistake continues to haunt you. You feel guilty that you spent so much on something that you never use. It is hard to take the first steps to get rid of the object, but once it is out of sight, just think of how free you will feel. You will no longer see that hideous vase in the dining room cabinet or the coat mistake in your hall closet. That guilt will be removed from your home and free you from object burden.

I think most people get caught up in object burden because they worry that Aunt Doris will notice the missing vase and be hurt. Or else they worry that others will see the mistake that was made in purchasing a bad item. I get it. No one wants to hurt someone else over a vase. However, you are allowed to live a stress-free life and if the items are burdensome, you are within your rights to eliminate the stuff. After all, the vase was a gift, freely given, and you are allowed to regift, donate or sell that vase to someone else who will really appreciate that item.

My husband feels guilty about getting rid of newer clothing that he rarely wore, but I simply remind him that those clothing items are perfect donations. People who need affordable clothing can go to the thrift store and get nice things that they would not normally be able to afford. This is a sentiment that you can keep saying to your collector family members who have trouble getting rid of items, even items that they never use or wear. Take your sentimental souls to Goodwill or other thrift stores and show them how good it feels to donate nicer items that people will be happy to find. People who collect things love to get good deals and find special items. Remind them that it is their duty to help provide that feeling to others when they donate newer stuff.

While I have less trouble getting rid of items that I never use, I have a harder time with handling bad decisions. I regret poor purchases or overpaying for items. If I make this type of mistake, I feel like I have failed the family by spending more than I should or wasting our resources. This is why it is the best decision to cut my losses and remove the item from the home. We all make shopping mistakes, and it is not worth keeping the item to try to validate its expense and existence. That ill-fitting coat is taking up valuable real estate in my wardrobe and making me feel bad. Therefore, it needs to go. Someone else might fit better in the coat and find it to be the perfect clothing item. In any case, I don't need to clutter my mind up with nonproductive feelings of guilt.

Other items that might be difficult to remove include sentimental family objects or handmade crafts. The general thinking is that someone made this item especially for me and I cannot disappoint that person. However, as a crafter myself, I know that I create things because it makes me happy. If someone doesn't want or need the item, I am perfectly happy for them to donate or give to someone else. I got the enjoyment out of making the quilt or tote bag. I do not want those items to become burdens to my kids or other family members. I regularly tell others to use the item if they want or to donate to someone else. If it helps lessen your object burden or feelings of guilt, then take a picture of the item, or write in a journal about the emotions that the object or giver inspires in you. You can also repurpose the item. Keep a scrap of the quilt your grandmother made you and turn it into a framed picture. My friend Amy took all the old-fashioned rings from her mother and grandmother and turned them into bracelet charms. She made the items more relevant to her fashion and, more importantly, had a nice memory piece to wear.

- **Lastly, it is just plain difficult to get rid of your own stuff.** A third-party bystander is always going to have a different viewpoint. I have a friend, Lori, ask me to come and help her organize her closet as it was bursting with stuff. Lori's daughter was in college and not in town to help her see what was fashionable and flattering. I was helping her out and we were going along swimmingly until we got to her several racks of black shirts. Lori called it her "Johnny Cash" wardrobe because she loved wearing black. I had already pointed out that as a beautiful blonde, she looked great in colors like ice blue and coral, and Lori had started branching out and getting a few new numbers in her closet. As we were looking through the piles of black shirts, it became clear to me that we could eliminate quite a few. Lori had duplicates of several items, some tops had faded to a weird gray-black color, and some were just dated and unflattering. We easily discarded about 20 tops but there were still too many shirts for the rack. I thought that we should get rid of another 20 just so the tops could reside on the rack comfortably and since there would still be over 60 black shirts, I thought that was more than enough to keep. After all, Lori probably still only wore the 20 most flattering ones on a regular basis! Lori let me help her decide on the next 20 shirts to go, but I could tell she was not happy with the process. While the first 20 easily went into the trash bag, she insisted on putting the next set off to the side. The next day she confided that she pulled 10 shirts out of the 20 set aside and stuffed them back into her closet!

It was easy for me to see what shirts needed to go for Lori, but just like everyone else, I often struggle with my own closet. It's funny how "what goes around, comes around." One Christmas vacation my daughters forced me into a blue jeans intervention in my bedroom. They poured out wine and then pulled out all my jeans and threw them on the floor. Then they mercilessly divided them into keep and discard piles. I was shocked to see that I owned over 40 pairs of jeans, even though I maybe wear jeans once a week. My girls pared it down to four pairs. Yep, FOUR! Then they let me haggle to keep two more, so then I was up to six. They reminded me that I rarely wore jeans and that I regularly wore the same ones that I found flattering. They made me try on the jeans that I thought I liked and then bluntly pointed out the flaws: they were baggy in the knees or too tight on the legs ("Skinny jeans are out," they exclaimed.). Now I know what I put Lori through in her own closet dismantling (Come to think of it, she has not invited me back to help, LOL!). Our stuff can be personal, and it can be difficult to visualize what other people see regarding our items.

Ultimately, Jan's relationship with her family is more important than decluttering. While Jan really wanted her parents to get rid of stuff and sell their empty home, she had to remember the importance of protecting their relationship. Again, it all goes back to developing trust with your chaotic family members, staying nonjudgmental and showing up "just to help" and not to take over. Admittedly, this is all easier said than done. There will be days that you get angry, bitter, and sad over the process, and that is okay.

Other situations that are stressful for us include getting divorced and moving house, especially if the decision to divorce or the decision to move has been forced upon you. These situations will, of course, require more grit and personal endurance than tasks like the joyful restructuring of your shoe rack and alphabetizing your mystery novels.

Death cleaning that occurs after a family member has died is even more traumatic, especially after an unexpected death when food is still left on the table and shoes are still by the doorway. This is when you want to gather support. Find loving friends or other family members who will come with you and be patient as you memorialize and grieve. In some instances, you might want to completely outsource the project and that is perfectly fine too.

Here are some ways that family members and friends can help you in any difficult and emotional cleaning process:

- Gathering boxes
- Packing up stuff
- Carrying
- Helping you focus and stay on task
- Providing a different viewpoint
- Consolidating items
- Listening to you describe your good memories
- Allowing you to cry over bad memories
- Encouraging you to finish the cleaning task to meet a deadline
- Taking over the project if that is the best outcome for you

CHAPTER 11 CHEAT SHEET

Things to consider in difficult organizational situations:

- For some people, especially those in older generations, the ability to get rid of items is thwarted by financial concerns.

- Some family members are more practical in their approach to stuff.

- A big clean up can be emotional since it represents the end of an era and a dismantling of goals and dreams that were established earlier in life.

- Getting rid of items can generate guilt in some of your family members.

- Lastly, it is just plain difficult to get rid of your own stuff.

- Consider enlisting help from others when you have to do hard tasks like clean out homes after a death, divorce or downsizing.

(12)

STAYING ON TRACK

My house is not perfect. There are several projects going on at once. I have been meaning to clean out the clutter on my make-up table for a couple of months now. In fact, my to-do list has "clean up make-up table" listed on it, and I keep ignoring the notation. My junk drawer has gotten a little crazy over the holidays with everyone digging into the space for batteries, Chapstick, Band-Aids and rubber bands. My box of aluminum foil got unrolled when we were baking cookies and is now haphazardly stuffed into my kitchen drawer along with a couple of near empty Ziploc bag boxes. The plastic containers that we use for leftovers are in several different places in my kitchen because the drawer where they should be kept also now contains cookie cutters and baking pans for some reason. I was busy at the beginning of January and all my Christmas decorations were just carried to the bottom of the basement steps and not packed away. And there's probably another hundred or so of these types of situations going on all around the house. But it's okay. I know about them. I will write them down at some point, and when a burst of energy appears—I will tackle them. Or when I can't find my tweezers, I'll take a half hour to reorganize my make-up area to better serve my needs. That is the ebb and flow of things.

So, here's the deal: we don't always do this organization thing perfectly. A lot of the ideas in this book might even go by the wayside in our household. Things get busy, someone goes off their medications, the holidays come in fast and suddenly all bets are off. Organization becomes hard again. But we never let go of that desire for order because we know that things go more smoothly when we have schedules. I liken it to my property rental business. We are only as good as our policies and procedures that we implement and follow. My employees are less stressed and more productive when they know what needs to be done and how to go about completing their projects. Your family is the same way. They will thrive with better schedules and guidelines in place, and they will be less stressed when they see the goals and know how to go about completing them.

The nature of our workdays has changed immensely, especially after the pandemic when many jobs turned remote, and we learned that a lot of productive work could happen outside of the office with great technological advances like Zoom and FaceTime. Everything has been further amped up by social media, and we often have no clear end to our workdays. Lots of folks are entering the gig economy and cobbling together a work career composed of two or three different jobs. Because of these many factors, it is more imperative than ever to tame the household chaos and get organized.

When organization is in place, your world will be more centered. You will have more time to just BE, to exist in the moment and enjoy the present. When clutter is under control, your world will seem calmer and less noisy. You will be able to compartmentalize better and keep the scary stuff at bay. You will be able to move around your home in peace, not worried that you have lost important things and not worried that your in-laws will pop in unexpectedly and see a terrifying mess. Your children and spouse will be empowered to improve their own organizational methods, and you will have stopped enabling them and doing all the hard work.

This is the vision: the harmonious home that is a haven from the rest of the world. It is the place you want to be after a hard day's work. It is the place you want to celebrate birthdays, anniversaries, and graduations. It is the place where you create, play, and relax. It is the place you share with the people you love most. So, it is worth the effort and the time that it will take to walk your people through the journey of becoming more organized and centered. When your procrastinators and ADHD people see progress and take control of situations, the excuses will no longer be relevant or necessary.

Once you get a few successes under your belt, you will feel better about the whole process. When your bedroom becomes a personal oasis, your garage now fits your car, and your children stop losing school papers, you need to remember to celebrate the progress. High five each other. Reward yourselves with ice cream. Reinforce the behavior that made these successes happen. You want the process to continue and improve.

Many people use the New Year in January as a starting point to get focused and back on track. Inevitably, right after the December holidays, all the podcasts, social media posts and TikTok videos highlight tips for goal setting, calendaring, and decluttering your home. However, you don't have to wait until January, and you don't have to jump on everyone else's bandwagons. It might not be the right time for your family, and it might not be the particular focus that you need. Just like everything else, there is so much noise out there on schedules, organization, and goal setting. And, of course, in this book, I just added to it all! However, I maintain that taking a more thoughtful and measured approach will create more change and be more successful than the information that you get in 30 second internet increments.

If you go online and do a simple search of "how to get my life in order," you will be inundated with a proliferation of ideas of how to get back on track. There are articles of 40 ways to get it together, 27 strategies to get your life in order, and so on. If you want to grab onto simple ideas like "write a to-list now" or "stop caffeinating your body," by all means, try these out. But if everything was so simple, we would all live in well-ordered homes and never be late for doctor's appointments.

So instead, if you get off track on this whole organized, well-ordered life thingamajig—simply STOP and take a deep breath. Get through the problems or situations that have arisen to make the family system get derailed. I'm guessing that those things are more important right now. Take the time now to just love each other. Reassure the ones who need reassurance, support the ones who need support, and accept help from others when you need that reassurance and support.

Then when those problems have gotten smaller or time has started to heal the pain, you can take the time to go back through this book and review different ideas. What worked? What didn't work? Find the strategies that motivated everyone and got them to declutter and get focused. Life is meant to be a nice long endeavor spent with loved ones and on projects or work that you find meaningful and rewarding. Don't complicate things or make them harder by imposing your beliefs on the rest of your family. Instead, do these things:

- Take time to figure out your family members' world views.
- Listen to your family members.
- Dream and strategize with your family members.
- Work together on goals and visions that empower each other.
- Reflect on what works and what does not work in your household.
- Repeat your successes!

This is the part of the book where I feel like I should leave you with an empowering message or quotation like "you got this" or "I believe in you." But that's kind of cheesy and, honestly, very contrived. Only you and your family can really fight the chaos in your household. Only you know the demons that wield power in your home. All I can leave you with is this: My family has had many demons. My family has known strife and turmoil. We have found ways to tackle jobs and get things done. We are not superheroes with superpowers. We are just ordinary people who have done some pretty cool things because we figured out ways to get through life. I hope our techniques will help you or, at least, give you some good ideas on what to do next.

I welcome your feedback! Check out my website at
www.askthelandlady.com
or drop me a message at askthelandlady@gmail.com.

Now, go hug your family members. Even if they are messy and disorganized procrastinators, collectors, and ADHDers—they are yours and you are theirs.

BOOK AND WEBSITE RESOURCES

Aarssen, Cassandra. *Real Life Organizing: Clean and Clutter-Free in 15 Minutes a Day.* Mango, 2017.

Allen, David. *Getting Things Done: The Art of Stress-Free Productivity.* Penguin Books, Revised edition, 2015.

Bologna, Caroline. (2021) "Why Millennials are So Into Collecting Things." *Huffington Post* [online] Available from: https://www.huffpost.com/entry/why-millennials-collect-things_l_61b80b36e4b-0911ceb59b49d.

Chapman, Gary. *The 5 Love Languages: The Secret to Love that Lasts.* Northfield Publishing, 2015.

Cherry, Kendra. "What is Revenge Bedtime Procrastination?" Verywellmind.com [online] Available from: https://www.verywellmind.com/what-is-revenge-bedtime-procrastination-5189591.

Davis, KC. *how to keep house while drowning: a gentle approach to cleaning and organizing.* S&S/Simon Element, 2022.

Durand G, Arbone I, Wharton M. 2020. *Reduced organizational skills in adults with ADHD are due to deficits in persistence, not in strategies. PeerJ* 8:e9844 https://doi.org/10.7717/peerj.9844

Ferrari, Joseph. *Still Procrastinating: The No Regrets Guide to Getting It Done.* Trade Paper Press, 2010.

FortyThree.me, www.FortyThree.me, Sim Technologies, 2023.

Hamdani, Sasha. *Self-Care for People with ADHD: 100+ Ways to Recharge, De-Stress, and Prioritize You!* Adams Media, 2023.

Hotchkiss, J. (2013) "How bad is our perception of time? Very!" *Huffington Post* [online] Available from: https://www.huffpost.com/entry/how-bad-is-our-perception_b_3955696.

Kondo, Marie. *The Life-Changing Magic of Tidying Up: The Japanese Art of Decluttering and Organizing.* Ten Speed Press, 2014.

Lembke, Anna. *Dopamine Nation: Finding Balance in the Age of Indulgence.* Dutton, 2021

Magnusson, Margareta. *The Gentle Art of Swedish Death Cleaning: How to Free Yourself and Your Family from a Lifetime of Clutter.* Scribner, 2018.

Mann, Merlin. *43 Folders.* 43folders.com, 2004.

Paston, Matt. *Keep the Memories, Lose the Stuff: Declutter, Downsize and Move Forward with Your Life.* Portfolio/Penguin, 2022.

Pinsky, Susan C. *Organizing Solutions for People with Attention Deficit Disorder.* Fair Winds Press, 2006.

Richardson, Kerri. *From Clutter to Clarity.* Hay House, Inc., 2020.

Robbins, Mel. *The Five Second Rule: Transform Your Life, Work, and Confidence with Everyday Courage.* Savio Republic, 2017.

Tank, Aytekin. *Automate Your Busywork: Do Less, Achieve More, and Save Your Brain for the Big Stuff.* John Wiley & Sons, 2023.

Tracy, Brian. *Eat That Frog!: 21 Great Ways to Stop Procrastinating and Get More Done in Less Time.* Berrett-Koehler Publishers, 2017

White, Dana K. *How to Manage Your Home Without Losing Your Mind.* W Publishing, 2016.

White, Dana K. *Decluttering at the Speed of Life: Winning Your Never-Ending Battle with Stuff.* Thomas Nelson, 2018.

Made in the USA
Middletown, DE
02 June 2024

54961098R00109